Hispanic Stars Rising

THE NEW FACE OF POWER

CLAUDIA ROMO EDELMAN

Hispanic Stars Rising

This book is a compilation of stories from numerous people who have each contributed a chapter and is designed to provide inspiration to our readers.

For more information, contact:

We Are All Human | www.weareallhuman.org
Hispanic Star | www.hispanicstar.org
Fig Factor Media, LLC | www.figfactormedia.com

Cover Design by Barbara Alvarez & Layout by Manuel Serna
Printed in the United States of America

ISBN: 978-1-952779-10-7
Library of Congress Control Number: 2020915514

I DEDICATE THIS TO MY LATE
MOTHER , CECILIA ROMO,
AND MY KIDS, JOSHUA AND
TAMARA, TO HONOR THE
EFFORTS OF THE GENERATIONS
THAT HAVE COME BEFORE US TO
LAY THE GROUNDWORK, AND TO
PREPARE THE WAY FOR THOSE
COMING AFTER US.

Table of Contents

ACKNOWLEDGEMENTS

I have to start by thanking my family. From being my daily inspiration, to giving me their unwavering support.

Thanks to everyone who worked hard in the production of this book. Special thanks to Jackie Camacho and the Fig Factor Media team who made this possible.

This book would not have been possible without the amazing co-authors who shared a deeply personal story that shaped them into the Hispanic Stars they are. You are an inspiration to all.

Words cannot express my gratitude to the publishers who donated their time and effort to make this book a reality.

To everyone in the We Are All Human team, thank you for making this and many other projects a reality, for being part of this amazing group, and for showing up every day and helping our Hispanic Stars share their stories.

FOREWORD

BY CLAUDIA ROMO EDELMAN

Hispanics are stars. I learned this after moving to America--the first time I realized I was Hispanic. I quickly recognized that our history is made up of extraordinary women and men who persevere through every obstacle and how we live by our values, passed on through generations.

I witnessed the resilience and passion that inspired me to advocate for the community I had just joined. However, I was also disheartened in the realization that this community suffers from what I call a 'reverse marketing problem.' As a marketer, you try to highlight the best attributes of your product, and in my previous career, I was doing this with global issues like poverty, AIDS, etc.

The marketing around the Hispanic community does the opposite. Our best attributes are often hidden or downplayed, while others tell our stories, control the narrative, and create a misconception of our strength and our importance to the U.S. The result is that we are often misunderstood.

Hispanics are powerful but are often portrayed as weak. We are huge but think small. We have been invisible, viewed as takers, and are overall negatively perceived. I'm a Hispanic living in America, and I take issue with the possibility that my kids will be paid less, underrepresented, and generally undervalued. This narrative is not only affecting the way Hispanics are seen in this country, but is also negatively impacting the confidence and growth of Hispanics themselves.

I looked at my children and realized that the time to act is now. The time for Hispanics to believe in ourselves is today. No more doubts.

This is our moment. We have never been so strong. We need to move from fear to action. We need to move from many to one-one unified community. By doing this, we will witness the transformation of our community, and we will flourish and thrive. I know it is possible.

And I'm not saying this just because I am a "super proud" Latina, I'm saying this because it's what the numbers and facts show. And let me tell you, in all the years I've been working for the United Nations, UNICEF, the World Economic Forum, and international organizations around the world, I've seen many communities thrive with less than what we have. I believe it's possible!

We are the people of America. We are the economic power. We are the youth. We are the entrepreneurs and the job makers. We're the consumers. And, we are growing--in numbers, in power and in strength. And we will continue to grow and succeed. Why? Because our values are strong. We believe in hard work. We are ambitious and professional. We are fighters, and we know how to overcome difficult situations. We are optimistic. We have a deep commitment to our family values.

We Hispanics are born to shine, so let's start controlling our narrative and highlighting our stories and our contributions. Let's finally show people who we really are. I'm absolutely convinced that we can be the last generation of U.S. Hispanics who are invisible, ignored, and undervalued. I want to see the next generation being fully paid, fully respected, and fully valued.

It's sometimes difficult to find what unites us. There's nothing easier than to dwell on the differences within the Hispanic community in the U.S. But, if you're reading this, it's because you believe in the strength, the power, and the beauty of our community. The fact that so much has been accomplished and that we are so strong is the result of decades of hard work and dedication by those who came before us, and our heritage that has shaped us into who we are.

I know we're ready to have our place at the table, to get the respect we deserve for our contributions to America, as one community and with one voice. But we have to understand that we are better when we rely on each other.

We need to realize that unlike what we've heard, the air is unlimited. There is space and air for all of us. We need to bust the bubble and come to this realization. Inside the bubble, we are defined by our own personal perspective: I am Mexican, I am Cuban, I am Dominican, etc. all fighting our individual battles. Once the bubble bursts, we will realize we all have a place here, and we can all participate in the promise of this country.

We need Hispanic leaders to step forward and speak up, not only about our strength, but also about our need to unify. About the imperative of not focusing on our differences but on our similarities in order for all of us to do better. We must start thinking as one powerful community because together, we are stronger.

Together, we are not a minority. We are a *majority.*

This book is full of incredibly inspirational Hispanic Stars who showcase the strength, resilience, creativity, intelligence, kindness, and passion of our community. It is my honor to share these stories with you as a source of inspiration, as a showcase of role models, and as a collection of true rising Hispanic Stars who exemplify the new face of power in the United States. I encourage you to take the time to read each powerful story, connect with the authors, and think about the significance of your own story as a Hispanic Star or that of the Hispanic Stars in your life.

–Claudia Romo Edelman

PREFACE

BY FONSECA

Being a Hispanic is being a star. More than 61 million stars shine every day in the United States of America. Stars that have dreams and work hard to accomplish them. Stars that have walked through long and hard paths to be where they are. Some of them take the wrong path, but a significant majority help this country move every day. No matter what, we are ready to work, and we always feel proud of who we are and where we come from.

I came to live in the United States almost nine years ago. I will always remember how I felt welcomed because of my music--because of its rhythm and message. That's my core, my culture. From that moment on, I understood that being Hispanic was almost as important as my last name in this country. People recognize you for that; it's your trademark.

Every time I hear a new story about a Hispanic rising star in this country, it inspires me. And I'm not just talking about the amazing 92 stories from all the Hispanic Stars that are part of this great book. I'm also talking about that lady that comes to the States from her home country, looking for new opportunities for herself and her family. That lady that comes to work legally, knowing that she will be away from her family for several years but determined to change her history in a country full of opportunities. She knows that her kids will have a better education because of her sacrifice and that she's changing the future of the next generation.

We all know a lady like this. That inspires me. Knowing that we as Hispanics have the strength to work for our future generations, even if we don't even know them. We know that working for our future is working for our home country's future as well.

We bring sensitivity in all we do--that's one of our most significant contributions. We, as Hispanics, have a unique way of feeling that is motivated by our country's history. We bring every scar of our people in every step we take. We can't hide our scars because they have made us warriors, and they are a very important part of our superpowers.

We have to be united now more than ever in history. We have to be proud of ourselves and what we've done because what we do generates positive effects in this beautiful country. That's why we have to see ourselves as stars that shine together as one.

I celebrate this amazing book because our Hispanic community's stories deserve to be seen, heard, and valued. These 92 stories will inspire lots of Hispanics, and, most of all, it will bring more awareness to the importance of what we do in this country. We work to make America inclusive, diverse, and beautiful. I'm sure that lady's son will one day be part of one of these 92 inspiring stories.

–Juan Fernando Fonseca

FOR ALL THE GIRLS WHO JUST WANT TO FEEL SEEN

MJ ACOSTA

"If everyone thinks your dreams are crazy, it means they're truly meant just for you."

The night of my first assignment as an NFL Network reporter, a man called out to me from the stands. I thought perhaps he wanted to know more about my interview with the star wide receiver. Or, maybe he wanted a selfie for his social media page. Instead, he asked me a simple question, "What is your curly hair routine?"

This man was a single father of a mixed-raced daughter. He had no idea how to manage or style her curly hair. "She saw you on TV reporting in front of the stadium and yelled for me to come into the room!" She had never seen someone who looked like her on TV before.

Like many Latinx households, my Dominican family had a post-dinner ritual which included gathering in the living room to watch the latest telenovela. I'd run into the room singing the theme song (my favorite part), and settle in.

But when we would gather to watch the beautiful people on the screen, I was always bewildered. I wondered why no one on the screen looked like me or my parents, even though we spoke the same language.

That was my introduction to the lack of representation for Afro-Latinos on the screen. After the telenovela, it was on to the nightly news, and you guessed it, there was no one who looked like me at the anchor desk either. All I saw were people with fair skin and straight hair on every Spanish language channel. It was no wonder that another mainstay for the women in my family was an obsession, nay, a responsibility to make sure our naturally curly textured hair or "pelo malo" was as straight as possible.

The more we could assimilate to the perceived standard of beauty, the better we would be received by society. This wasn't out of malice, but rather out of survival. My family was taught this was the way to a better and more successful life, and they wanted the same for me. But, the generational traumas of our ancestors were manifesting themselves in a fashion where our roots, our blackness, and our Afro-Latinidad was being suppressed to the point of delusion.

It took nearly 30 years of exhaustive soul searching and self-acceptance to get to a point where I could proudly embrace my natural curls. I call my curly afro "Angela." She's not my alter ego, but rather my inner self finally out to the world in the form of a curly crown for all to see! My curly crown is a symbol for little girls who are longing to feel accepted, loved and represented. I am that little girl who felt like her dreams were too outlandish because there was no one I could look to as an example.

I learned that if everyone thinks your dreams are crazy, it means they're truly meant just for you. I am here as proof for all the girls who just want to feel seen.

BIOGRAPHY

MJ Acosta is the first ever Afro-Latina reporter and host at the NFL Network. Fully bilingual in English and Spanish, she contributes to shows such as *NFL Total Access, NFL GameDay Morning, NFL Now*, and across multiple platforms for NFL Mexico and NFL Español. MJ started her career in local news covering sports, entertainment, and hard news in Miami, Florida, and San Diego, California. Early on, MJ graced the sidelines as both a reporter and a Miami Dolphins Cheerleader. In her nearly decade-long career, the Emmy award-winning journalist continues her work as an advocate for representation and equality. MJ works closely with women's empowerment groups such as A Seat at the Table, and is dedicated to amplifying the voice of marginalized communities.

FROM DUST-FILLED STREETS OF RURAL ARGENTINA TO DARTMOUTH, TO DEMOLISHING IT ALL

VALERIA ALOE

"And from this clean slate, my purpose was born: to make it all about them and not about me."

My journey started in a small, agricultural town in rural Argentina. In this town of unpaved streets, my father did not attend high school as he became the main breadwinner at the age of 11. My mother did go to high school, but college was beyond what her family could afford.

From a young age, I stood out as a brilliant student, which later on attracted all sorts of bullies. The same qualities that singled me out as my family's hope of the first one to attend college, became a curse in high school. A stranger in my own land, I counted the days to start a new chapter, called "college."

At the age of 18, I packed my bags and moved to Buenos Aires where, I am not embarrassed to admit, I had to learn how to cross streets with traffic lights and ride buses.

Two college degrees later, both with honors while working full time to pay for my studies, I joined Procter & Gamble after a series of never-ending interviews. Checking out this new world, I kept my humble beginnings and my limited world exposure a secret as I sat in huge conference rooms with super-smart kids coming from the top educational institutions in the country.

Fast forward a few years, after chasing a dream of higher education in a foreign country, I would be landing at JFK International Airport with my husband, tons of bags, and limited savings, to pursue an MBA at Dartmouth. A summer job at McKinsey was followed by years in corporate America with leading roles and huge responsibilities, compensated with business-class trips to Europe and tempting year-end bonuses.

But the small girl that ran in the dust-filled streets of rural Argentina, who overcame all sorts of obstacles and limiting beliefs about herself--without role models--was ready for the next adventure, or better yet, a shake-up, as she made herself heard with a major burnout in 2016.

Surrounded by walls I had built to protect her from feeling like she did not belong, the little girl stood up and demolished the illusions of recognition, money, and degrees to ask the one question that would change her life forever, "Why am I here, and how can I serve?"

And the answers came flooding in, in gigantic waves that would tear down those walls, demolishing them all. And from this clean slate, my purpose was born, to make it all about them, and not about me...and to support minorities and immigrants who are the first ones in their families to dare to dream of creating an extraordinary life.

There cannot be any substitutions for who you are meant to be. The time has come for Hispanics to awaken to our true individual and collective purpose, and live from our authentic, extraordinary, powerful inner selves.

BIOGRAPHY

Valeria Aloe is a minority development expert and leader with more than 25 years of professional experience in Fortune 500 companies (Procter & Gamble, Reckitt Benckiser, Citibank, TIAA-CREF, McKinsey & Co, and others), start-ups, and nonprofits, across multiple industries, in seven different countries, and in three languages. As the director of entrepreneurship for the Hispanic Chamber of Commerce of New Jersey, she has helped hundreds of business owners achieve success and prosperity.

An award-winning entrepreneur, she is also the creator of *Abundancia Consciente, the Science of Extraordinary Results*, a research-based, behavioral change, bilingual platform that guides participants to manifest extraordinary achievements from the true self.

MY EMPOWERING JOURNEY

ARABEL ALVA ROSALES, J.D.

"We have the power to create a life that can positively impact others while at the same time fulfilling our dreams."

My parents immigrated to the U.S. from Mexico and met in Chicago, where our family was raised. The Mexican traditions were deeply embedded, and we could only speak Spanish at home. I was raised knowing I would get married and have children, like my mom. Dinner with our family included dad hosting a question and answer session that would shame Jeopardy, and it included self-development and the idea that with clear visualization, clear intent, and hard work, I could do and be anything, like my dad.

Our family lived in Pilsen, then Little Village. Both were tough neighborhoods. Yet school, sports, and involvement with our entrepreneurial family was all-consuming. My dad was a tailor-turned-designer, marketing his designs via his TV program, one of the first in Spanish in Chicago. Early on I understood cross-marketing, and the importance of community involvement.

While graduating high school, I prayed for a job where I could help a lot of my people. A few days later, I landed a job in the governor's office as an administrative assistant. I knew no one in politics, but I just jumped right in. I decided to say yes, I can, then figure it out.

Working my way through college, I became a top advisor to then Governor Jim Edgar, and found that I was also good at politics. Finishing my undergraduate degree, I was appointed director of the Liquor Control Commission. By then I had gotten married, had a beautiful daughter, and started pursuing a law degree. Ending my term, it was time to go back to my entrepreneurial roots.

I launched AAR Tech, creating a company that uses tech tools to successfully manage large institutions. Tech was different back then, but I knew in my gut that it was the way of the future. Gladly, both my business and I have successfully evolved over the years.

My life, personal and professional, went through some transformational and tough times. My dad died, I graduated law school, became a single mom—it's a long list. Difficult times prepare you for the big opportunities. And being successful in business allows you to pursue your passions while earning a place at powerful tables. *Chicago Magazine* described me once as a "new age renaissance woman" because of my ability to understand finance, global issues, and my love of art and fashion. I love being involved in organizations where I can truly have a positive ripple effect on society, especially in the Latino Community.

Through Latino Fashion Week, and recently through RUNWAY LATINx, I have created a fashion platform that is known in the major cities of the U.S. and Latin America. By launching Pivoting in Heels through its digital platform, we have further fueled the importance of empowering women. I proudly share with my daughter, a fellow first-degree black belt in Tae-Kwon-do and recent University of Michigan graduate, that we have the power to create a life that can positively impact others while at the same time fulfilling our dreams.

BIOGRAPHY

Arabel Alva Rosales, J.D., is president & CEO of AAR Tech, a company with over 15 years as a leader in management and technology tools. She serves on several boards including currently serving as Interim Chair of the Chicago Transit Authority (CTA), Chair of the IHCC Foundation Board, and Director on the WBDC board. She is a leader in the fashion industry as founder of Runway Latinx (your fashion wk), the previous co-founder of Latino Fashion Week, and the founder of Pivoting in Heels, NFP, the digital non-for-profit she has created and dedicated to the empowerment of Women. Arabel is a first-degree black belt in Tae-Kwan-do, earned an undergraduate degree from Loyola University, and earned her Juris Doctorate from DePaul College of Law.

ONE MAN'S JOURNEY TOWARD THE GALAXY OF STARS

DR. JUAN ANDRADE, JR.

"Success is not measured by how high you climb, but by how wide you reach."

Success is not a destination, but a journey. My journey officially started in September 1970, 50 years ago. I was recruited right before graduation for a teaching position in Crystal City, Texas. My activism experience was a baptism by fire. Racial tensions were running high in Crystal City after a walkout involving 1,700 students who were protesting unfair school policies.

My first day was a transformative experience. I was a Civics teacher, so I started my first day with the Bill of Rights. About halfway through class, I started sensing that many of my Mexican American students were not grasping what I was trying to teach. I stopped and asked how many students were understanding what I was teaching. A few Mexican Americans and all the Anglo students raised their hands. I asked those who didn't raise their hands if they would like for me to repeat the lesson in Spanish. They all said yes, so I did, and felt really great. I did it again on the second day and felt great again!

My third day started with a knock on my door. It was my principal. He informed me that the police were at the school to arrest me and were waiting in his office. Apparently, I had violated state laws that prohibited the use of any language other than English, in any classroom other than a foreign language classroom. The police said I could teach that day if I would turn myself in after school. I agreed, knowing that my teaching career would soon be over.

That afternoon, I broke the law again and became a fugitive from justice. My lawyer was in San Antonio, so I had to wait for him. (In Texas, it's not wise for Mexicans to go to court without a lawyer.) The school board president, my principal, and I hid out in the City Manager's office, across the street from the courthouse. Unbeknownst to us, my lawyer went straight to the courtroom and told the judge where we might be. The police arrested me at City Hall and drove me to the courthouse.

In court, I pleaded not guilty. The plan was to force a conviction so we could appeal to a higher court, and eventually get the laws declared unconstitutional.

The plaintiffs, the Concerned Citizens Council, figured out our strategy and dropped the charges because if I won, teachers all over Texas would be speaking Spanish in their classrooms. Still, the seeds of change were planted.

My teaching career ended in December, after one semester. The Texas legislature later repealed the law, and teachers who could do what got me arrested were paid a bonus. Victory follows sacrifice. I realized then that success is not measured by how high you climb, but by how wide you reach.

I started a new job in Milwaukee in January 1971, and immediately joined a peaceful march. The police turned it into a riot, and my journey found its purpose. I would spend the rest of my life trying to change the world, for the better.

BIOGRAPHY

Dr. Juan Andrade Jr. is the fourth Latino in history to be honored by both the President of the United States and the government of Mexico. He earned five degrees, and received five honorary doctorates and three distinguished alumnus awards. Recognitions include Chicagoan of the Year, Lifetime Achievement (three times), *One of the 100 Most Influential Hispanics in America* (five times), *Un Orgullo Hispano* by Univision, and honored by most Hispanic magazines. Since 1982, he has served as president and Executive Director of the United States Hispanic Leadership Institute. The only Hispanic commentator on radio and television, and a newspaper columnist as well, he has helped promote democracy in 10 countries.

BREAKING BARRIERS: MI CAMINO ADELANTE

EDUARDO ARABU

"Si Se Puede."

My life journey begins on another continent, as I was born in Caracas, Venezuela. After a few years, my parents decided to immigrate to the U.S. and we settled in Chicago, Illinois. As a young child, I managed two cultures and two languages. I learned Spanish at home while learning English at school. I was always exposed to cultural diversity as my neighborhoods, schools, and environments were filled with individuals from all over the world. I was a good student, testing ahead of my grade level, and playing sports.

After grade school, I was admitted to Lane Tech High School, one of the city's most selective schools and among the top 100 in the U.S. I opted for the Army's Junior Reserve Officers' Training Corps (JROTC). As a cadet, I learned discipline, followership, communications, leadership, and teamwork skills which shaped my character development.

I completed my JROTC term as a cadet captain. Simultaneously, I was also a cadet in the U.S. Air Force's Auxiliary–Civil Air Patrol--where I quickly rose to cadet major. However, as graduation approached, I struggled with mentorship, access, and resources for college and career development.

After two years at odd jobs, I was hired for a human resources role at a food manufacturing company. My supervisor encouraged me to explore the Northeastern Illinois University (NEIU) El Centro program for non-traditional and returning adults. It was at NEIU that I acquired my first two mentors who were instrumental in my academic development and resulting career opportunities.

I enrolled in evening classes while working full-time and was able to complete my Bachelor of Science degree in business administration. I was the first in my family to graduate from college. I worked for the Ounce of Prevention Fund, the office of an Illinois State Senator, and Schawk, Inc. I was elected to serve as president of student government and student trustee. I led several teams to Model Illinois Government and Model United Nations.

To date, I've earned numerous internships, scholarships, fellowships, leadership positions, awards, and other recognitions worth over $175,000.

Today, as executive director of the National Hispanic Corporate Council (NHCC), I am advising corporate America on their Hispanic market strategies. Corporate engagements with NHCC are designed to enhance the Hispanic talent, consumers, suppliers, community relations, and executive development strategies of American companies. I worked with globally recognized organizations and brands to help educate decision makers on the impact of the U.S. Hispanic community that is 60 million individuals strong and $2 trillion in purchasing power.

I share my story because, to quote the Hispanic Star Initiative, *"America is made up of stars, Hispanics are one of them. Hispanics in the U.S. should be seen, heard, and valued. Our stories must be told and showcased. We are Hispanic Stars."*

Individuals face challenges and barriers; however, there are resources (often not enough) that exist to help our community. With determination, commitment, and goal setting, ***"Si Se Puede."***

I dedicate my success to all the Hispanic Stars in my life–my family, mentors, and professors.

BIOGRAPHY

Eduardo Arabu has experience with corporations, nonprofit organizations, educational institutions, sport entities, and governmental agencies. Most recently, he worked for the United States Chamber of Commerce, the Chicago Cubs baseball organization, the office of a U.S. Representative, the office of an Illinois State Senator, and several corporations. Eduardo has earned numerous internships, scholarships, fellowships, leadership positions, awards, and other recognitions.

Eduardo also earned a B.S. in business from Northeastern Illinois University, completed a management fellowship at George Washington University, and received a M.S. in public policy and management from Carnegie Mellon University.

EL PENDÓN ESTRELLADO

ROGER ARIAS

"Our National Anthem, in Spanish, preserved in intent and history for las gentes valientes en libre país."

El Pendón Estrellado, the official U.S Spanish translation of *"The Star-Spangled Banner"*, was "lost" for decades and would most likely have remained so but for pure serendipity.

In 1945, the Division of Cultural Cooperation of the Department of State called for submissions of Spanish translations of *The Star-Spangled Banner*. Translation is easy; making a translation singable is not. The Peruvian immigrant and composer, Clotilde Arias, proud of her new country, took on the task. Her son, Col. Roger F. Anduaga-Arias says he recalls her spending many hours seated at her stand-up piano, playing to the lyrics as she wrote and rewrote them.

Her efforts met with success and on May 16, 1946, Clotilde received a letter from the Office of the Secretary of State indicating that her work had been accepted as the official translation of the national anthem. *El Pendón Estrellado* was subsequently employed as part of a United States outreach, in friendship, to the Spanish-speaking countries of the Americas. Clotilde died in 1959 with her translation largely unknown in the U.S.

In 2006, Roger F. Anduaga-Arias II, Clotilde's grandson, was in Argentina presenting a business opportunity to Exxel Group and Indiecito Studios. During a break, the conversation turned to a discussion of the lyrics of Nuestro Himno which had been published by one of Exxel Groups relations, Adam Kidron. Adam Kidron's, *Nuestro Himno*, Spanish for "Our Anthem," was an unfaithful translation of *The Star-Spangled Banner*," favoring style over accuracy. The choice of lyrics for this translation of the national anthem was generating considerable publicity and promulgating controversy. Remembering stories I had heard about my grandmother translating the anthem, I surprised everyone when I said, "My grandmother, Clotilde Arias, wrote the official Spanish translation of *The Star-Spangled Banner*. This precipitated introductions to Adam Kidron.

Upon my return to the U.S., I searched through Clotilde's documents, locating not only Clotilde's handwritten notes, but all three translated verses of *The Star-Spangled Banner*" as well as the U.S. Government letter of acceptance and documentation on her payment. Wanting to "set the record straight" on the Spanish translation of the national anthem, I wrote to Adam Kidron sending some images of the documents.

Adam Kidron, the CEO of Urban Box Office, met with me in New York City, Clotilde's home. During this meeting, Adam told me that he had been contacted by the Smithsonian concerning *Nuestro Himno* and gave me his Smithsonian contact information. Adam said he knew the Smithsonian would be very interested in the official Spanish translation of *The Star-Spangled Banner*.

My subsequent dialogue with the Smithsonian culminated on September 29, 2012, when *El Pendón Estrellado* was sung by Choral Cantigas at the opening of "Not Lost in Translation," a Smithsonian biographical exhibition of the life of Clotilde Arias. Our National Anthem, in Spanish, is preserved in intent and history for *las gentes valientes en libre país.*

The Arias family is pleased that *El Pendón Estrellado*, beautifully sung by Jeidimar Rijos, is accessible to a wider audience thanks to its release by the We Are All Human Foundation (WAAH) on YouTube.

BIOGRAPHY

Roger Arias is the oldest son of a French/Spanish family. Through family circumstances he learned hard work, perseverance, and thrift. He put myself through school, graduating with a B.S. in business management. Roger proudly served in the U.S. Army, and is the co-owner of Screaming Games LLC, a developer of mobile games for iPhone and Android.

CULTURE SHOCK AND THE UNWRITTEN RULES

VICTOR ARIAS, JR.

"No hay que llegar primero, pero hay que saber llegar."

Growing up in El Paso, Texas, was an incredible privilege. The border and its bicultural nature are a beautiful laboratory of co-existent experiments with the Mexican and U.S. citizenry all becoming one melting pot. Everyone, regardless of ethnicity, is Latino. That was my experience being raised by two wonderful parents whose heritage came directly from the state of Chihuahua. My first language was Spanish, and my customs at holidays are purely Mexican. I still love menudo, tacos, and churros, yet enjoy a good hot dog and brew at football games. My parents and grandparents taught me the value of respect for others, to keep an eye on the end game, and appreciate the paths blazed by those who came before.

When I left college at University of Texas at El Paso (UTEP) and went to the Stanford Graduate School of Business (GSB), it opened up my world. I learned a lesson that has been instrumental in approaching life: I learned that I really was Latino or Mexican (others would remind me), yet I downplayed that. My first experience at Stanford, a place I had never visited before, was a wine and cheese reception (what is that?).

I dressed up in my fashionable velour sweatpants, my best-looking Texas baseball cap, and new Nike tennis shoes. Already feeling intimidated, I walked into the courtyard and I felt like I had neon lights shining on me amidst this preppie crowd. One gentleman came over and we had a wonderful conversation. He took me over to meet his new friends. They were great people and I had to change the pronunciation of my last name to make it easier on them.

The last guy in line was a six foot, four-inch tall, sandy-blonde gent with thick, brown corduroy pants, boat shoes (I learned later they are called Topsiders), two golf shirts with alligators on them with the collars up, and what looked like a mandatory blue sweater draped over his shoulders. I introduced myself. He kind of grunted, and I said, "Let me turn down your collars." I did, and his face turned beet red as the other six people laughed and thought I was being courageous, when I was just trying to be helpful.

Those six people became my best friends, and that gent never spoke to me in those two years. Oh, well, that is an example of culture shock, but also shows that with a strong sense of confidence and being respectful, things turn out just right. These are the many life lessons that "just happen."

I have served on the boards of organizations like the Stanford Board of Trustees and a public company board (Popeyes). I have co-founded various organizations, including what is now called Prospanica, the Latino Corporate Directors Association, and most recently, the Stanford Latino Entrepreneurship Association. My current work as an executive recruiter is about IMPACT...creating more opportunities for better governance and, in many cases, more Latino directors. I am thankful for the guidance I received early on to keep your eye on the end game.

As Alfred Jimenez says, *"No hay que llegar primero, pero hay que saber llegar."*

BIOGRAPHY

Victor Arias, Jr., is the Managing Director at Diversified Search Group and has more than 25 years of experience in executive search. Specialties include board of director placements, and he has been very involved with the Latino community on the board of the U.S. Hispanic Chamber of Commerce, co-founder of the Latino Corporate Directors Association, The Alumni Society, Prospanica (co-founder of NSHMBA), on the board of the Notre Dame Institute of Latino Studies, and co-founder and board chair of the Stanford Latino Entrepreneurship Initiative.

Victor is a retired board member from Popeyes, a trustee emeritus for Stanford University, and a former appointee as a White House Fellows Commissioner.

He holds a bachelor's of business administration from UTEP and an MBA from Stanford.

THERE'S NO TURNING BACK - NOT EVEN THE SKY'S THE LIMIT

LISETTE ARSUAGA

"Rise and rise again until lambs become lions!"

I grew up in Puerto Rico and lived there until I went off to college at age 18. Until then, I wasn't defined as Latina, or a minority. I was a girl, a teenager, an aspiring woman. I was a person who had no limits because no limitations had ever been imposed upon me. I was defined by my character and convictions because I had not been labeled or stereotyped by something other than my own accomplishments and sense of purpose.

That changed once I moved to the U.S. The aperture by which I saw my life was suddenly constricted by others. I was defined not as a woman, but as a Hispanic/Latina. I was not only judged by my actions, but by the actions of millions of others who were also defined as Latinos/as. As a young woman, entering a world different from the one I grew up in, I was forced to reassess where I fit in and how I would be able to effect change.

I soon found myself fighting stereotypes and preconceived

notions of what being Hispanic meant. I decided to change the conversation, enlighten those who knew no better, fight for equality, and against discrimination/hate. I first did this as a political consultant in my early 20s, then as a change agent for human rights organizations and non-profits nationwide. Ten years ago, when opening my own company, DMI-Consulting, with my husband and partner Gilbert Dávila, I brought my passion and experience to the marketing/advertising industry.

Gilbert and I launched DMI-Consulting at a time when 2010 census numbers were coming out, and companies were realizing that in order to grow–and even survive–they had to be more inclusive. The fact that, for example, Hispanics were growing exponentially faster than any other segment could no longer be denied. Since then, we have been fortunate to work with some of America's top companies. One of the most rewarding experiences of my career is as a co-founder of AIMM – the Alliance for Inclusive and Multicultural Marketing, founded in 2016.

The year AIMM was founded was key, as it was an election year, and one in which we witnessed a divisive nation like we'd never seen before. We saw an opportunity to bring together the marketing and advertising industries in order to instill a much-needed message of unity and inclusiveness.

Today, AIMM has more than 100 companies representing Hispanics, Blacks, Asians, LGBTQ+, and people with disabilities. We have brought together marketers, advertising agencies, media and research companies, and non-profits to work collaboratively towards the prioritization of diverse segments to maximize business growth.

Throughout my career I took "no" for an answer too many times, but I never gave up. As a strong Latina, I pledged to "rise and rise again until lambs become like lions." As lionesses protect their young, it's time we protect our own by forging a path that's free of discrimination.

Like me, today my daughter is defined as an aspiring woman–a Latina. My goal is to make sure that for her, being Latina means the doors of opportunity are opened wide, and I intend to open doors for all Latinos, so together we can forge ahead into a better world.

BIOGRAPHY

Lisette Arsuaga is the co-president of DMI Consulting, which she founded in partnership with Gilbert Dávila in 2010. As the co-founder and head strategist for DMI, Lisette has provided strategic guidance for companies including McDonald's, P&G, AB, Kimberly-Clark, Kellogg, Proactiv, Gatorade, Dunkin' Donuts', Marriott Hotels, New York Life, Aetna Insurance, A&E, Ulta Beauty, and SeaWorld, among others. She is also co-founder and board member for the ANA's Alliance for Inclusive and Multicultural Marketing (AIMM), bringing together 100+ corporations, agencies, media/research companies, and trade associations to address challenges in the multicultural media, advertising, and marketing space today, including the representation of Latinos in programming and advertisement.

IN THE END, EVERYTHING I DO IS CONNECTED WITH THIS PURPOSE

ROSARIO B. CASAS

"I am obsessed with finding more women and Hispanic talent using technology to solve the biggest problems humanity has - AKA sustainable development goals."

When I was a girl, I dreamed of being President of Colombia, building a better future for people. That's why I started studying political science with a major in economics.

After years of following that route and working in the government (Anti-corruption Presidential Program and Chief of Staff for a Colombian first lady), I realized the importance of entrepreneurship as a key part of economic development. I decided to pursue an MBA, and in 2009 jumped to incorporate Business Creative Partners, developing a consulting method to attract and land foreign direct investment operations.

One day, back in 2013, I was contacted by Senseta, a Silicon Valley startup building state-of-the-art big data and artificial intelligence solutions. They were acquiring a small Colombian company and were looking for M&A advisors. My company was contracted, and after some months they gave me an offer to be their global CEO. I am one of the first Latinas appointed as a CEO for a big data/AI company, replacing a founder after opening a Series A.

That opportunity opened my eyes, and I realized the power of exponential technologies to scale solutions. I fell in love with technology and its possibilities, and, for the first time, the topic of being a woman and a Latina was mentioned in conversations with business peers and superiors. I learned English as an adult and, of course, a strong accent is one of the elements that made it obvious, but for me that conversation also opened a window to see the gap in perception about Hispanic talent. That also provoked my curiosity, and I decided to start learning about technology and software development.

Two years later, I left the company and my husband was appointed to work in NYC. We moved together, and when I was making the decisions on what to do, I told my husband, "I can go back to finance, but should take certifications that could take me around two years, or I can start a new technology company." He knew what I was saying. "You already know what you want! I am ready to give you my support," he said.

Seven months later we started XR Americas with my co-founders, Lucas Kappaz and Tom Herman. After five years we have a solid role in the immersive technologies landscape. In 2017, I was named one of the 100 Top World Disruptors in NYC by the World Summit on Innovation and Entrepreneurship, and in 2019 named *Mujer Legendaria* by Ford Motor Company and one of the 100 OBO Movement Innovators of 2020. I am obsessed with finding more women and Hispanic talent using technology to solve the biggest problems humanity has – AKA sustainable development goals.

I earned seats at key tables in the technology and startup environment, and I can call myself a serial entrepreneur and developer. Now, my motivation is to use all these foundations to help women and Hispanics to assume a role in tech building while I keep creating solutions for global critical problems. I am living my childhood dream from the private sector, building solutions instead of policies.

BIOGRAPHY

Rosario B. Casas is co-founder of XR Americas, a NYC-headquartered company that uses spatial computing for workforce skills development, Business Creative Partners, and BCPartnersTech, a company who is leading digital adoption and transformation.

She is obsessed with finding more women and Hispanics using technology to solve key global challenges, is the co-creator of the Four-Dimensional Quotient Discovery Guide and is a co-founding member of Dreamers & Doers, a private collective of entrepreneurial women turning mutual support into a competitive edge.

She is also an advisory board member at Rutgers University Big Data, WE NYC Mentor, SXSW Pitch, XR In Learning, and TWIN Global Tech. She is an entrepreneurial mentor at Tandon School of Engineering at NYU, the Founder Institute, and a TEDx speaker.

GRACIELA BALMORI

"Even the most daunting situations can be resolved by taking one step at a time."

"My dad died, didn't he?" My son approached the brightly lit doorway as his 11-year-old, small-framed body wailed in distress. The universe had chosen this dark, solemn, and moonless night to be a witness to our despair. His eyes met my grieving eyes and confirmed what he already knew, without me ever uttering a word. His father had passed away just hours before.

It was late and I had just arrived after making a same-day round trip from San Francisco to Houston, never having reached my destination in Mexico. Sorrow greeted my four children, who had been kept painstakingly busy throughout the day until I came home to deliver the most devastating news.

My ex-husband was an addict and had long suffered from alcohol and drug abuse. Overdosing, alcohol poisoning, blackouts, and ICUs had been "our normal" most of our married life. When

I got the call to fly to Mexico where he had gone to spend the holidays, I felt certain my care, like many times before, would nurse him back to health.

Since I bought my ticket late, I was assigned a seat in the very last row. I hadn't slept the night before, so I dozed off to the rumble of the engines.

An hour before landing, my eyes sprung wide open as I felt my heart leap out of my chest, inexplicably pounding rapidly for the next several minutes. Frantically, I began to pray. Upon landing, I called my sister-in-law, and when she picked up the phone she simply yelped out, "He is gone!" I searched every face in the plane, trying to make a connection. "Help me! Something horrific has just happened in my life!" All I wanted to do was fall to the ground and bawl, but I couldn't.

I was alone with my anguish. I sat there quietly weeping and waited for every single person to leave the plane as they struggled to unwedge their bulky luggage. When it was finally my turn, I paused. Certainly, this heart-wrenching circumstance deserved an uncontrollable outcry of emotion. It was the least and the most my body could do. I was, indeed, physically and emotionally alone. At that moment, I decided to rely on courage to help me get through, even when I didn't have the strength to go on. I stood up, grabbing the back of the seat in front of me to pull myself forward. I looked down at my feet and forcefully told them to move one in front of the other.

Even the most daunting situations can be resolved by taking one step at a time. With each step I thought about my past, present, and future. I knew my past life was gone and my future had been changed forever, but at this moment I had to intensely focus on the present and my next couple of decisions to help me and my children get through this. Simply placing one foot in front of the other helped me get out of the darkness and begin my transformation towards a more purpose-driven life.

BIOGRAPHY

Graciela Balmori has had 16 years of success spearheading strategic business development in beauty, jewelry, and health and wellness. As an associate partner at Ameli Global Partnerships, she applies coveted knowledge in helping organizations create inclusive strategies to drive increased market share from both corporate and consumer perspectives.

As a Latina executive who holds a seat at the table, she now lives her life by paying it forward. She has helped 100s of women feel inspired to dream bigger by tapping into their cultural assets and what they are innately capable of accomplishing to gain more socioeconomic capital and decision-making power.

TRUST THE PROCESS

RUTH BATRES

"Each struggle lived defines our character. You are exactly where you need to be, believe in yourself and trust the process."

"Ruth, just trust the process," are the words that I hear inside my head every time fear and frustration try to take over me. Life never came easy in the place where I grew up, Ciudad Juarez, Mexico, known as the most violent city in the world.

Multiple family members and close friends were victims of the sex-based hate crimes against women known as femicide. Afraid that I could be next, my mother decided that moving to the United States would be the best decision, and in 2005, at the age of 13, my family and I migrated to Los Angeles seeking safe haven.

The American dream seemed so unattainable. I cried every day, begging my parents to please take me back home. I did not speak a word of English, and I had no place to call home. My undocumented status made this process more difficult. It was during my senior year in high school that I realized how difficult life was going to get.

Keep going, I would tell myself. Although life felt so overwhelming, I made the conscious decision to hold on to something that I could control--my education, which is the main reason why I decided to enter the world of academia.

I had no idea of how I was going to make it, but I was always willing to take that next step. I got through community college by working two jobs and organizing many fundraisers to pay for tuition. It was here that I became an advocate for myself and the dreamer community. I wanted to be the voice for those that felt voiceless, as I once felt when I first moved to this country.

After all the sacrifices and hard work, I was able to transfer to my dream school, the University of California Los Angeles (UCLA), where I did my research about violence against women in my hometown, Juarez. I told myself that each struggle lived defines our character. You are exactly where you need to be, believe in yourself, and trust the process. Despite my undocumented status, I also had the opportunity to study abroad in Brazil and finish my degree on the other side of the equator.

Pursuing higher education was something that I always wanted to do. I had no money and no documents, but I decided to just trust myself and apply for that master's program anyway. Two years later, I found myself graduating with a master's in guidance and counseling, one of the best decisions of my life!

I now look back and I am so happy that I did not let fear take over, and that I always took that next step, regardless of how difficult life appeared to be. Currently, I work as a counselor and help dozens of people daily to trust themselves and the process of life in order to keep achieving their goals.

I am a big believer that each struggle we live is required to become the best version of ourselves that we are meant to be. This is my fuel to keep going every day and smile at life, even when things get difficult. I just remind myself to trust the process without hesitation, because what is coming is bigger and better than what I have already.

BIOGRAPHY

Ruth Batres is a DACAmented Scholar and Community Activist born and raised in Cuidad Juarez, Mexico. Ruth and her family fled their country because of violence and arrived in Los Angeles, where she has been residing since then. She attended UCLA and obtained a Bachelor of Arts degree in international studies and earned a Master of Arts degree from Loyola Marymount University in counseling and guidance. She currently works as a vocational rehabilitation counselor for L.A. County, as well as an academic counselor for the community college district. Ruth's ultimate goal is to one day become a college president and create a non-profit organization for the undocumented population.

THE POWER OF HUMAN CONNECTION

MICHELLE ENOJI BEATO

"There's an opportunity waiting in every conversation you invest in."

I was still a curious journalism student when my love of coffee and conversation helped me land my dream job. I became an assistant producer for Univision Network's national morning show, *Despierta America*, before I graduated college. I was working as an intern at a local Univision station when I built a connection with a frequent show guest via early morning coffee chats. One day she informed me that a position at the network morning show had opened up, and that she could recommend me. Weeks later, I interviewed for the position and was offered the job. I couldn't believe it!

I admit I wasn't prepared to walk into a fast-paced office full of journalists, producers, and cameramen, working non-stop. My job was to find unique, human-interest stories for us to feature on the morning show. There was definitely lots of pressure, especially since

I had limited experience and this challenge required me to speak and write in Spanish, which I wasn't used to since I was part of the first generation in my family to be born in the U.S. I immediately began looking for stories to feature and quickly tried to acclimate myself to the new environment.

During this time, I attended a Marine Corps ball in Atlantic City with a friend. This is an annual celebration that commemorates the founding of the Marine Corps. I began having conversations with many of the Marines that evening and was fascinated by their stories.

A few weeks passed and I got a call from one of the Marines who I had connected with at the ball, and he made me an unbelievable offer. He asked if my team and I would be interested in going to Parris Island, the home of the Marine Corps Recruit Training Camp in South Carolina, to observe the experience for ourselves. What!? I brought this idea back to my team and we unanimously agreed it would be an amazing opportunity.

We were escorted by Marines to Parris Island and spent three days observing all of the different activities in boot camp and interviewing recruits of Hispanic descent. We filmed a series of raw and emotional stories of the struggles, challenges, and triumphs that bring recruits to the decision to become a U.S. Marine. We laughed, cried, and cheered them on to graduation. We came back and turned the footage into a series of stories for the morning show.

It was an incredible experience that turned into one of the most important and memorable opportunities in my career as a young inexperienced producer trying to prove herself. Since then,

I've continued to use the power of connecting with others to build my career.

There's an opportunity waiting in every conversation you invest in. I owe my first dream job, and every opportunity afterwards, to investing in my relationships with others. Every person has a unique story and when we invest in connecting with others, a world of opportunity will open.

BIOGRAPHY

Michelle Enjoli Beato is a bilingual speaker and career coach who teaches strategies on how to connect to career and business opportunities. She was a first-generation college student who got her dream job while she was in college, and since then has worked for global brands in television broadcasting and marketing.

WHAT SUCCESS MEANS TO ME

KARINA BERMEO

"True leadership requires courage, passion, and is difficult, but not impossible."

I grew up in Guayaquil, Ecuador. I went to college, and at the same time I worked to pay for my studies, got a business degree, got married, and had two wonderful children.

I had a good life there. I lived in an apartment with a beautiful view of the entire city and had a successful corporate career. As a former Fortune 500 executive with a strong track record of more than 15 years of experience building and managing successful negotiations with financial institutions, defining success seemed quite simple. It was another step up in my career ladder, a salary increase, more people reporting to me, and a place on the board.

However, while I seemed to be doing well, my career progress didn't make me happy. I was losing connection with my self-identity. Sometimes I merely pretended to be happy, with a smile painted on my face. It was at that moment when life gave me the great challenge of leaving everything and making the decision to move to another country, where I did not know anyone, the language, or its culture.

I was fearful. Why should I give up on my ambitions? As it turned out, leaving my country was one of the best decisions I ever made because it helped me to discover my call, my passion, my essence, and what success means to me.

I decided to become an entrepreneur with the fervent desire to work and serve my community. It was a great opportunity for me to show what I was capable of doing in a short amount of time, and without capital. For me, this was a challenge as well as a great opportunity because I never worked in communications.

I overcame the challenge by getting clear about the goals I wanted to achieve for myself and my community. As a result, I created a media company with a purpose. I provide information, support, and empowerment, and helped businesses harness social impact and diversity, equity and inclusion (DE&I) into Hispanic communities.

New York City is my home now. Being present in our community is one of the most important parts of my job, and what I'm passionate about. Maybe for a business or a person, it seems easiest to define success in the number of social media followers, web visitors, or the amount of money they make annually, but other signs of success excite me much more. I feel happy and energized when I can help my community achieve its goals. I feel passionate, proud, and inspired to help my clients find their writing voice, share their ideas, and discover the joy to serve the community with their gifts.

The mark of a great leader is someone who leads by example and embodies their company's character. True leadership requires courage, passion, and is difficult, but not impossible. I feel happy when I can find the right balance between work and relaxation and take time to care for myself. Feeling at peace and excited by my work may seem a modest form of success, but it's huge for me. I look forward to continuing the progress made over the next few years.

BIOGRAPHY

Karina Bermeo is a former Fortune 500 executive with more than 15 years of experience and a strong track record of building and managing successful negotiations with financial institutions. She was president of the Sabmiller Foundation, and in 2015, arrived in the U.S., with her two children, a suitcase, and did not know English.

By 2017, with her experience and passion for serving, Karina had inspiration for Hispanic America. She provides information, support, and empowerment to her community by helping businesses to harness social Impact and DE&I.

She is also an award winner and a motivational speaker for conferences and middle and high school students.

NEVER STOP RE-INVENTING YOURSELF!

BETSABE MARTINEZ BOTAITIS

"Be resilient- every person has failed until they succeed."

In the fall of 2015, I enjoyed working in finance at a company on the verge of IPO. My partner and I had just purchased our first home and could walk to work. I was expecting my first child. The pregnancy was a happy surprise after having been told by multiple doctors that I was not able to get pregnant. Years of hard work and passionate dedication to my career and personal life were coming to fruition.

And then, everything changed. On that clear and crisp November day, I went to my OB because I knew something was wrong. An exam showed that I was in labor much, much too early in my pregnancy– only 22 weeks. I was immediately admitted to the hospital.

Over the next five days, the doctors and I did everything we could to preserve the pregnancy and the precious life. My daughter was born at 23 weeks, weighing only 1 lb. 8 oz. Over the next three months, I would return to work while spending every moment I could at the NICU. Every day was a new challenge; my heart broke with each setback and soared with each gain. Through all this, I never gave up on my child or myself. I reinvented myself, gaining confidence while advocating for my daughter.

Finally, happily, I brought my tiny daughter home. The child thrived. So much so, that when my career took me back to Guadalajara, my daughter became an international traveler.

The dangerously premature birth of my daughter made me focus on seizing the opportunity in front of me. Always one to take calculated chances, I drove myself to reach for the stars that were further away and harder to claim. I sought more challenging career opportunities, knowing I could handle anything the job threw at me.

As I say, "you need to ask for what you want--whether it's information, assistance, or opportunity. And, you keep asking until you get what you need."

Even as a girl in a traditional Mexican family in Guadalajara, I forged my own path, rejecting my expected role and began working in a bank as a teller before finishing high school. I learned that creativity, resilience, and confidence were and continue to be essential skills to move up the ladder within a very male dominated and class driven culture. It's important to be resilient--every person has failed until they succeed.

After coming to the US and obtaining my MBA, as a new immigrant and Mexican female, and with a strong accent, I found it incredibly challenging to gain meaningful employment. I knocked on a lot of doors before finding one that I could walk through--at Citigroup.

Confidently making my own path, I haven't stopped knocking on doors and moving forward. I have worked in increasingly larger roles at a pre-IPO company, a fintech start-up in Mexico, and a blockchain startup.

BIOGRAPHY

Betsabé Martinez Botatis is an accomplished strategist and fintech executive, currently leading the finance team at Uplift. She has over 15 years of experience ranging from large financial institutions, fintech companies to a blockchain startup.

Prior to joining Uplift, she held various senior positions at renowned and leading-edge companies including Kueski (Mexico's largest fintech startup), Lending Club, and Citigroup, at Citi Community Development and Financial Inclusion.

Betsabé also served on the advisory board of the Nasdaq Entrepreneurial Center, is a fellow for the British America Project, and is a member of Hipower, a network of executive women leaders laser-focused on accelerating one another's success.

TIME, TALENTS AND TREASURES

MARIA CASTRO

"We all have them, so let's share them."

With over three decades of experience within different industries, I can proudly say that I have secured my seat at the table to help organizations and young up-and-coming. Latinos take a leading role in society.

I am the proud daughter of Jose Reyes-Maltos and Maria Oralia Cuevas-Maltos. My dad was a migrant worker turned entrepreneur. Born and raised in south Texas, he and mom met in second grade and eventually married right out of high school. Our roots in Texas go back multiple generations to the mid 1800s.

I was born and raised in Chicago's Pilsen community and am the youngest of four. I attended private school and focused my sights on poetry and drama in school. Growing up in the 70s wasn't easy for a person of color. My first jobs would prove to be challenging in the banking and legal industries. I worked hard and hopped from job to job until I landed a position in the radio industry. Working at

Spanish radio stations in the 80s was very difficult but prepared me for a long-term career in the retail marketing field.

Eventually, I found myself working as the director of marketing for a shopping center on Chicago's north side. After honing my marketing skills there, I moved on and accepted a position as a regional marketing director, overseeing eight shopping centers. I continued to work as a consultant for national event marketing companies, which led me to my current position 15 years ago.

Today I am the regional external affairs manager at Comcast in the Greater Chicago region. This is exactly where I was meant to be, helping our most challenged and vulnerable communities with corporate investments such as grant support, event sponsorships, affordable internet service and scholarship awards. It has given me the opportunity to bring resources back to where I grew up.

I believe we all have time, talents, and treasures, so let's share them! By doing so, I have received numerous awards and acknowledgements for my community service work including a proclamation of *"Maria Castro Day"* in the City of Aurora, (Illinois' second largest city), among many others.

I am refer to myself as a *"CEO of Inspiration."* Serving as the chairperson for the Hispanic Scholarship Fund's Chicago Chapter, the advisory board of the Women's Business Development Center, the board of directors for the DePaul Art Museum and the Telemundo Chicago Action Board Committee. I have participated as a speaker for the first live Latina Talks in the Chicago area and at the *New York Times* in New York City. I am a co-author of *Today's*

Inspired Latina Volume V and *Today's Inspired Leader Volume II.*

On the personal side, I am the proud wife of Martin Castro III, and mother of two sons, Martin IV and Phillip, mother-in-law to two daughters-in-law named Jessica, and grandmother to Savannah, Martin V, Amaya, Aaliyah, and Adrian.

#ThePowerOfUs
#TogetherWeAreStronger
#TogetherWeShallRise

BIOGRAPHY

Maria Castro is an experienced professional in the areas of community investment, CSR, and corporate event planning. She is a co-author of *Today's Inspired Latina Volume V, Today's Inspired Leader Volume* and Latina Talks speaker (New York Times & Chicago). She serves as chair of the Hispanic Scholarship Fund Chicago Chapter, is on the Women's Business Development Center's Advisory Council, the *Telemundo* Chicago Community Action Board, and the DePaul Art Museum board of directors.

Maria has received numerous award acknowledgements: *Negocios Now* 2019, Who's Who Hispanic Chicago, 2019 Aurora Regional Hispanic Chamber of Commerce Hispanic Catalyst Champion, YWCA Women of Distinction Award, People with Disabilities Champion Award from Seguin Services, Corporate Visionary award from El Valor, 2020 Hispanic Style Latina of Influence, and the 2020 *Today's Inspired Latina* Woman of the Year Award.

UN LIDER JOVEN: A YOUNG LEADER

BRANDON CISNEROS

"Don't do it for the paycheck, do it for your last name."

Perth Amboy is a small city in the central region of New Jersey. The community is predominantly Hispanic/Latino and lower middle class. There are a lot of cultures represented here with people from all over Latin America, such as Ecuador, Mexico, Guatemala, Peru, Dominican Republic, and Puerto Rico. Growing up, I never truly embraced my culture, and I was slightly privileged compared to many of my friends.

Throughout high school, I wanted to become more involved with administration and be a voice for the students. I served as president of student council for two years and was student representative on the Board of Education. Within those roles, I advocated on certain issues that students wanted addressed by administration. One of my proudest achievements was instituting an academy model that revolutionized our way of learning. These academies focused on specific fields of studies to help students discover what they were interested in so they could gain more practical skills before graduation.

I moved to Philadelphia to pursue my studies in marketing at Drexel University. Here, I noticed the vast difference between my school and Perth Amboy. The student population was mostly Asian or white, with an extremely small Latinx community.

During my time at Drexel, I joined cultural groups such as Latinos for a United Campus to socialize with other Latinx students. I became involved in professional organizations such as Prospanica, ALPFA, and the Greater Philadelphia Hispanic Chamber of Commerce. As a member of these organizations, I networked with countless individuals who helped me advance my career. I started with Prospanica Philadelphia as a volunteer on the marketing committee and became the marketing officer in 2019. After serving the professional chapter for two years, I made the decision to start my own university chapter. Prospanica Drexel became the first and only university chapter in the Northeastern region, and we quickly grew.

Because of my passion to give back to the community and embrace my culture, I came across the Hispanic Star campaign. There was a national call to establish hubs in cities to make a significant impact on the Latinx population in the United States. I stepped up as the leader of the Philadelphia Hub.

As the youngest leader for the campaign, I am humbled and honored to be a part of something that makes such a significant impact to the Latinx community in Philadelphia, as well as the nation. We have raised money for students affected by COVID-19, we had a webinar series to provide professional development skills and resources, we are planning to host donation drives for local nonprofits, and we are planning a collaborative event for Hispanic Heritage Month in September.

I am grateful and proud of where I am today and I couldn't have done it without the support from my family, friends, colleagues, professionals, and more. I have been inspired and live by this quote from former PepsiCo Latinx executive Richard Montañez: "Don't do it for the paycheck, do it for your last name." I am a Cisneros and I am a Hispanic Star in action!

BIOGRAPHY

Brandon Cisneros is of Ecuadorian and Chilean descent. Originally from Perth Amboy, New Jersey, he currently lives in Philadelphia. He is pursuing a bachelor's degree in marketing from Drexel University as a first-generation student. As a young leader on and off-campus, he advocates for the Latinx community by providing opportunities and resources. Along with the Hispanic Star campaign, he is involved in Prospanica (The Association of Hispanic Business Professionals), Bienvenidos (Drexel University's Latinx Faculty/Staff Employee Resource Group) and serves as a student ambassador for the university working with the admissions team on diverse student recruitment initiatives.

REMOVING THE MASK OF INAUTHENTICITY

ELIZABETH COLÓN

"To be yourself in a world that is constantly trying to make you something else is the greatest accomplishment."

We are pleased to announce that you have been selected as the Small Business Person of the Year for the State of Illinois (2014), you are the recipient of the 2015 Women in Business Award by the National Association of Women Business Owners (NAWBO), you are receiving the 2017 Latina in Business Award by Negocio Now. And the list goes on and on! Amazing, right? Not quite.

I never imagined, as a child growing up in a single parent household on government assistance, that I would overcome the constant struggles my family and I faced. My mother, who only had a second-grade education, never encouraged us beyond finishing high school, getting married, or simply working. I did exactly what she preached, and I got married at the early age of 18 and started working. I never considered going to college until I was 23, when my ex-husband encouraged me to do so. My struggles did not end there. I eventually became a single mother, and my dreams of finishing school vanished.

Being that I married so young, I wanted to experience the fun times I missed. My circle of friends had no ambition or desire to excel. By this time, I was exhausted and tired of the life I was living. I never had enough money to pay my bills, my car got repossessed, I dated the wrong men, and I constantly felt like a failure. I lacked confidence in myself because I thought I was not good enough or smart enough for anything beyond what was in front of me.

Words are powerful, impactful, and they will destroy you inside and out. I never knew what it felt like to believe in myself, to be myself, until I decided I wanted my life to change.

I cut ties with all my friends and started envisioning the life I wanted. I began to journal, meditate, and surround myself with positive, encouraging people, a new tribe. Although I thought I had arrived at my forever place, I crossed paths with someone who once told me that I needed to work on myself. Her comments resonated with me and I started to reflect on what was missing. It came down to not being authentic! I pretended to be something I was not, and this was the missing piece.

This journey led to living the best version of myself. I've discovered that to be yourself in a world that is constantly trying to make you something else is the greatest accomplishment. After years of battling with the negative voices and beliefs, I realize that all the awards, acknowledgements, and opportunities were meant for me because I have the gift of being a giver, a servant leader, and a visionary.

Today, I am the president and founder of an award-winning language service company called Metaphrasis Language & Cultural Solutions, and the first ever Latina president for NAWBO Chicago. I am proud and honored to hold these titles, and to be able to propel other women to higher grounds.

As Latinas, we are raised to believe that certain things in life are not meant for us and therefore we have to follow the old traditional rules. Wake up each day and live purposely your authentic self. Remove the heavy mask and flow graciously as the person you were meant to be. Abrazos!

BIOGRAPHY

Elizabeth Colón is a speaker, contributing author, philanthropist and CEO of the award-winning language service company, Metaphrasis Language and Cultural Solutions, LLC.

Growing up in a home with two deaf sisters and parents who spoke very little English, Elizabeth saw the many ways that language can become a barrier for individuals who do not have the means to communicate on their own.

Her experiences inspired her to become a language advocate and provide a voice for individuals who may not have the means to communicate on their own. In the spirit of giving back, Elizabeth is currently the board chair of the Norwegian American Hospital Foundation and was recently installed as the first Latina president of the National Association of Business Owners (NAWBO), Chicago Chapter.

BE BETTER, NOT BITTER

BETHANY CRUZ

"You see, God puts you in the right place at the right time. You just have to recognize it and be open to learning from the experience."

I recently discovered an enlightening way of looking at things, called Reverse Gap. The goal is to feel gratitude for your journey by looking back at how far you've come. While reflecting on it, the word that comes to mind is resilience. It's what made me who I am. During my lifetime I've endured experiences that I am saddened to say are far too common in society. My story is nothing new, and I'll bet that most people can relate to it in one way or another.

I have always needed to be helpful. Initially, I thought it was because I was the eldest of five children to an emotionally unavailable and poor mother. However, I now see that it's because I was destined to break the cycle of abuse and trauma that plagued my family long before I was placed on this earth. Because of my grandmother's life's circumstances, her pessimistic view of the world was passed on to my mother. The mentality was, "It's good enough for me. It's good enough for you." In reality, we should want more out of life.

I didn't always feel that way though. I was pregnant by 16, and a mother to three young children by the time I was 23. My highest aspiration at the time was to issue driver's licenses. I believed if I could do that I'd be set! Thankfully, God had other plans for me.

I went to work for a staffing agency that placed me in a sales office of a hotel. I worked alongside people who talked about their college life and seeing their degrees hanging from the wall made me reevaluate my own life. Their children had nice things, while I scraped by not knowing how I was going to feed mine. Instead of being bitter about why I had been dealt this hand, I looked at it as a lesson. I wanted to feel a sense of accomplishment. I wanted the feeling of financial security. That inspired me to start and complete my higher education.

It wasn't always easy. I worked days and attended classes at night while balancing my responsibilities at home. Luckily, I had the support of my husband and family, or I wouldn't have made it. It took me ten years to get my bachelor's degree, and right before finishing my final semester, God opened an opportunity to me as a health educator. The only qualification I had was my willingness to learn and a can-do attitude. A few years later I obtained an MBA and built programs that serve others.

I can't believe how far I've come. I wake up every day feeling two things: a sense of satisfaction with where I am in life, and happy that I can help make people's lives better. My family isn't perfect, and because of the work I put into bettering myself, I know that future generations will benefit from the cycle I broke. Statistically, I was on track to fail because of where my life started. As I analyze my past, I see how every difficulty, every turn, led me to where I was supposed to go. You see, God puts you in the right place at the right time. You just have to recognize it and be open to learning from the experience.

BIOGRAPHY

Bethany Cruz lives in Houston, Texas, with her husband of twenty-four years and three children. She has a bachelor of psychology from the University of Houston-Downtown, and an MBA from Our Lady of the Lake University.

Currently, she works for a large transplant center where she created an initiative to increase living donor awareness for patients needing a kidney transplant.

Bethany says her purpose in life, "Is to inspire others by teaching them how to live a better quality of life."

DIFFERENCES ARE A GIFT

PATRICIA DELGADO

"Only you have the power to embrace your differences with the courage to make your mark."

It was a sunny day in my beautiful hometown of El Paso, Texas, when I attended my senior year college fair. I walked to each table to gather information and from the corner of my eye, I noticed an unfamiliar college in Minnesota. I thought to myself, Wow, that's far from home. After speaking with the college representative, I became very interested.

I ran home and told my mom about it. After a strange look, she asked me, *"Y por donde es eso?"* I pulled out a map to show her where Minnesota was and later chose to attend the college. The school covered my tuition and gave me a work-study job. With all the bravery and excitement in the world, I left home to start my journey.

When I arrived on campus, I noticed that nobody--and I mean nobody--looked like me. My counselor then kindly welcomed me and said, "You can start your day at the multicultural center with the other students of color." I looked at her with surprise and confusion. I thought, *Me? I'm a student of color? What does that even mean?*

As I walked into the room with students of all different races other than Caucasian, I realized what she meant. That day I learned I was a person of color. My unawareness of racial identity was innocent since I came from a predominantly Hispanic community who didn't talk about race. Later that day, I was told about the student Latino house, the Black house, and a Chinese house. From that day on, I felt different. One day, listening to a Selena CD, I heard a loud voice. It was a Latino student who yelled, *"Que onda."* You should have seen my face; it was like I had seen Santa Claus. I later met other Latino students, and I finally felt a bit at home.

The semester began, and I could feel my courage slowly disappearing. I was stared at, treated differently by peers and professors, and asked if I eat beans and tacos every day. I decided to live in the Latino house my second year and shield myself from the main campus. Eventually, the idea of being different became too much to handle and I decided to return to Texas.

Reflecting back, I realized my thinking was all wrong. Being a woman, a Latina, and different, makes me AMAZING. The words, "person of color" are only words. I should have never let anyone, or any circumstance, doubt my abilities and identity. Only you have the power to embrace your differences with the courage to make your mark. I should have never let my uncertainties guide my decision to leave the college.

Today, I embrace my differences with courage and pride, knowing they are a gift. I later graduated from the University of Texas at El Paso, went on to get my master's degree in liberal studies, organizational leadership, and I am now completing my doctorate in psychology with a focus on industrial organizational psychology. So, remember to never doubt yourself. Lead with love, courage, and always *"Echale Ganas."*

BIOGRAPHY

Patricia Delgado (PsyD candidate) is an experienced industrial-organizational psychologist with a research focus on Hispanics in the workforce. As a proud Mexican American, Patricia was born and raised in the Texas border town of El Paso.

Patricia applies her cultural qualities and academic competencies to enhance awareness about the Hispanic population. Her advocacy and commitment to the advancement of the Hispanic population stem from her personal experiences with the challenges and successes depicted with people of color.

Patricia will continue her work to educate and promote the Hispanic population's commitment, work ethic, uniqueness, diversity, and love for family.

SOÑAR NO CUESTA NADA

IVONNE DÍAZ-CLAISSE

"Challenge yourself to achieve the seemingly impossible."

I will never forget the first time I formally shared my story with young students. I was visiting a school in Newark, New Jersey, as part of my employer's community outreach efforts. In the large school auditorium, looking at each one of the students' faces, I saw so many young Latinos who reminded me of myself. It reminded me of my dreams and doubts as a young girl growing up in Caguas, Puerto Rico.

I talked about the obstacles I faced as a shy student with a passion for math. Though I struggled to muster the confidence to raise my hand in the classroom, I eagerly completed my math homework after school. As I got older, I challenged myself by taking the most advanced math classes available. There, I faced not only more difficult content, but also teachers who doubted my ability to master it.

One teacher told me that as a woman, I would never be as

good at math as my brother. The comment stung—but only for a minute. Instead of taking his words to heart, I focused on proving them false. And I succeeded. I aced the class and got accepted into the University of Puerto Rico to study mathematics.

Though I faced similar challenges in college—professors and peers who saw a woman, a Latina, and discouraged me from pursuing an advanced degree—I found a role model in a Puerto Rican professor who had earned his Ph.D. in mathematics in the United States. Inspired by his journey, I went on to earn a master's in engineering from Cornell University, a master's in mathematics from the University of Maryland, and a Ph.D. in mathematics from Arizona State University.

My story struck a chord. After I finished, students lined up to get my autograph!

I was stunned by a simple yet profound realization. *I could be the role model I once looked so hard to find.* My words could give young students the inspiration and encouragement that would have meant so much to me at their age. I also knew there were many Latino professionals like me who could share their stories and show students that they too could achieve their dreams if they worked hard and stayed in school. This idea led me to leave my 10-year career in the corporate world and lead the nonprofit HISPA (Hispanics Inspiring Students' Performance and Achievement) in 2007. Today, we have reached more than 15,000 students.

My mother told me at a young age that *"soñar no cuesta nada"*, to allow myself to dream. And not only dream, but challenge yourself to achieve the seemingly impossible. I overcame the challenge of being one of the few Latinas studying mathematics.

I came to the United States to pursue every educational opportunity available to me. And I left the comfort and safety of a career, risking everything to do what I knew in my heart was right--help students dream of a better future and become the best possible versions of themselves.

BIOGRAPHY

Dr. Ivonne Díaz-Claisse is founder and president of Hispanics Inspiring Students' Performance and Achievement (HISPA), a nonprofit that mobilizes Latino role models to inspire Latino students to pursue higher education. Founded in New Jersey in 2008, HISPA expanded to Texas in 2011, New York in 2013, Florida in 2015, and Pennsylvania in 2019.

Under her guidance, HISPA has earned numerous awards and has reached over 15,000 students. Dr. Díaz-Claisse holds a B.S. in mathematics from the University of Puerto Rico, a master's in engineering and mathematics from Cornell University and the University of Maryland, respectively, and a Ph.D. in mathematics from Arizona State University.

CULTURE IN THE WORKPLACE

KARINA DOBARRO

"I am proud to say that I help brands connect authentically with consumers through culture."

Right now, I call New York City my home, but I was born in Buenos Aires and grew up in Honolulu, Hawaii. As a first-generation college graduate, I attended San Francisco State University and majored in international business and marketing. I always knew I wanted to work in advertising but did not know exactly what area to focus on.

When I graduated, there were not very many entry-level jobs in the industry, however I was not about to let that stop me. I sent my resume to over 100 companies, and I got a call back from just one media agency called Initiative. I was there for two years before being promoted, and later transferred to their office in New York.

I spent seven great years at GroupM agencies, until I joined Horizon in 2014 where I launched the multicultural practice. Within five years, Horizon was the third largest Hispanic media agency in the United States. I then became the U.S. lead of Local Planet, which is our international network of independent agencies. I still felt as though I could play other roles within Horizon and sought more responsibilities.

I became a member of the agency's Diversity, Equality and Inclusion (DEI) Council, along with launching Horizon Unidos, a Hispanic-focused business resource group. Having to manage all these roles can be challenging at times, but never impossible. It is what I enjoy and what I am passionate about–it is what makes me strive to be the best that I can be.

At Horizon, a recent project that I have been excited about and very proud of is our partnership with Pitbull, to launch 305 Worldwide! This new agency will serve as a liaison between media, content, and creative, through a multicultural first approach. My role at 305 Worldwide is Chief Strategist, where I will aid in bridging the two agencies together. I am thrilled by this collaboration, and I know that it will allow more multicultural consumers to feel included and celebrated.

I can't tell you how personally fulfilled I am to be doing what I love. To be able to work in advertising, while also advocating and celebrating my culture, is truly a blessing. There are many businesses and organizations today that only think of multicultural as an afterthought and not a priority. I am proud to say that I help brands connect authentically with consumers through culture.

As a first-generation Latina, I have achieved so many of my goals and I continue to work hard to get where I want to go. Like many other Hispanic Stars, nothing was ever handed to me.

Through support from my family, friends, and mentors, I was able to get to where I am today. However, I am far from finished. There are many projects I want to start, people I want to meet, and dreams to achieve. My journey continues…

BIOGRAPHY

Karina Dobarro is Head of Multicultural at Horizon Media. With 15+ years of experience, Karina joined Horizon in 2014 to launch the multicultural practice. She leverages her extensive knowledge of the U.S. multicultural market to develop comprehensive marketing strategies for clients.

She is a member of Horizon's DEI Council where she facilitates agency events and partnerships to support the advancement of diversity efforts within the agency. She has been honored by Adweek as a Media All-Star, by Cynopsis as a Top Women in Media, and this fall will receive the Executive Leadership Award at the Annual Hispanic Television Summit.

A COUNTRY WHERE I FOUND A SECOND HOME FULL OF OPPORTUNITIES

SANDRA ESCALLÓN

"I found ways to open doors and do what I love the most."

My name is Sandra Escallón and I was born in Colombia. I decided to come to the United States when I was 21 because I wanted to learn English, and at the same time I had a desire to experience another culture. New York City was a city that welcomed my dad a long time ago, before I was born.

He told us beautiful stories and the magic behind the Big Apple, and I wanted to explore it and live it. When I decided that I wanted to travel to the United States, my mom and my dad supported me, and they helped me to find a way to do it.

Unfortunately, my mom, the woman I love the most, passed away because of cancer a couple months after we were looking. It was really hard, and I miss her every day, but she became my angel, and I feel she has been with me during my journey and is somehow helping me to open doors in this country.

I came as an au pair, and I had the good fortune to live with a beautiful family that became my angels and support in the United States. Within a year, I received an opportunity to go to school, and my life started to change in a beautiful way.

I studied communications at Montclair University, and after I finished, I gradually gained experience for my career. I was alone, without connections, which made it difficult at the beginning, but I found ways to open doors and do what I love the most. There were months when I did not have anything, but I kept going because I had dreams, and one of them was showing the beauty of the Latino community throughout my skills and stories.

I started to volunteer at events where I could get experience as a journalist, and little by little, I started to get to know people and covered events that represented the Latino community and its culture, which is the topic I am passionate about. I was one of the few journalists who were covering events from a high-level, where there was a representation of our culture or stories from our countries.

Thanks to my work, discipline, trust in God, and love for what I do, I was able to get jobs that I love, and work in my field in a beautiful way. I have already won awards and recognition for my work, and I write and record stories that show the beauty of culture and the good in people.

I thank life and God that in this journey of more than 10 years I have found beautiful people to help me and had life-changing moments. Even though I miss my family and my country, I now feel more connected with them and with myself.

My journey continues and I am happy to see how far I have come. I am a proud Latina and a Hispanic Star.

BIOGRAPHY

Sandra Escallón is an award-winning, bilingual journalist based in New York City. She graduated from Montclair University with a major in communication studies and has experience as a writer, journalist, digital producer, social media producer, reporter, and blogger.

Sandra has worked with TELEMUNDO 47, *HITN, HispanoPost, HOLA! USA, NY1 noticias, My LifeStyle Magazine* and others. Sandra was also the press representative/public relations specialist for World Music Boutique Productions and Daniel Fetecua Productions, and worked as a press officer for The Colombian Film Festival.

Some of the events that she has attended and covered are The Colombian Film Festival, New York Fashion Week, and Tribeca Film Festival. She has also interviewed artists such as Calle 13, Hans Zimmer, and JR.

For Sandra, believing in her dreams, listening to her heart, God, and love are the key to overcome any obstacle.

FORCE FOR GOOD AS FORCE FOR GROWTH

JERONIMO ESCUDERO

"So much good happens when you set an audacious goal and get to work with passionate people."

How can the private sector act as a force for good for Latinos in America? This is a question I asked myself many times throughout my career in Procter and Gamble, in my early days working in the newly formed Multicultural Business Development Organization (MBDO), while leading the Pampers NA business, where 25 percent of births were of Hispanic descent, and then even more prevalently as I led P&G's efforts to develop content and capabilities to help brands reach and resonate with Hispanic consumers.

I am now convinced corporate America has a responsibility to help Latinos thrive and in doing so will have a major impact on their well-being and also create massive wealth to fuel our country's growth for years to come.

With my conviction, but little experience with how to get started, I met We Are All Human (WAAH) and their Hispanic Star platform. I was inspired by their mission and knew P&G should take a leadership role in supporting it. Then COVID-19 hit, forcing us to adjust strategies.

As COVID spread, I quickly realized the need to help Latinos was urgent, and that P&G could leverage its resources to provide help with relief and recovery. However, agility and speed are sometimes a challenge in large corporations. My experience in manufacturing and brand management taught me we needed to do things differently, and that is exactly what we did.

I created an internal COVID-19 USH relief/recovery taskforce and partnered with WAAH, Circulo Creativo, national relief agencies, and other stakeholders. Within weeks, this one-of-a-kind team created a complete intervention ecosystem that helped drive visibility to the urgent need for help in USH communities, amplify the impact of Hispanic Star's Month of Action by raising donations and providing essential products and PPE to families in need, and inspire employees and P&G brands to get involved in relief and recovery related activities.

The work was not easy and working across different functions and organizations remotely made it particularly challenging. Yet, we somehow found a way, inspired by our manifesto, trusting each other in our areas of expertise, focusing on the biggest opportunities, and staying connected for fast decision making.

As I reflect on the work done, I realize how much the experience has opened my eyes to what is possible. I now understand how fundamental it is to create partnerships between corporate America and non-profit organizations to drive meaningful, long-lasting change. So much good happens when you set an audacious goal and get to work with passionate people.

I am particularly grateful for the opportunity to collaborate in the "Estamos Unidos" manifesto. All people involved in creative development were Latinos, which is rare. The work helped us take the first step in our journey and act as a catalyst for long- lasting transformation within P&G by jumpstarting employee engagement, including the creation of a Hispanic Star Hub in Cincinnati, and the infrastructure and systems to connect national relief agencies with Hispanic Star Hubs. It also provided the opportunity for individual brands to get involved with product donations and support. Best of all, we are just getting started. Helping Hispanics help America.

BIOGRAPHY

Jeronimo Escudero leads Procter and Gamble's (P&G) efforts to reinvent media through consumer data and digital technology. He is currently leading company-wide efforts to modernize how P&G brands collect, analyze, and use data for stronger brand building.

He is a passionate advocate for equality and inclusion, playing a leadership role in P&G's U.S. Hispanic employee resource network, responsible for shaping P&G's efforts as a force for good towards U.S. Hispanics, and strengthening integration with P&G categories and external stakeholders. He also leads efforts to advance recruiting, retention, and talent development for the brand function.

Jeronimo currently lives in Cincinnati with his wife and three daughters.

MY JOURNEY TO BECOMING A BUSINESSWOMAN

ARACELI ESPARZA

"A woman who writes has power, and a woman with power is feared." -Gloria E. Anzaldúa

Being a creative individual comes with many strengths. We are natural connectors, visionaries, and innovators. We see the big picture, but often we second guess ourselves, because we connect the dots effortlessly. As a woman of color and first-generation college graduate, we walk through the world with a vulnerability that makes our journey so engaging and human.

This vulnerability is also our weakness. We give away our ideas with a hope and not a business contract. In our vulnerability, we get into unproductive negativity that drives people away when we need people to help us.

In my journey discovering my brand and business, I tried many different hats. I tried the yes hat because saying yes to everything will help me gain the right connections, right? I tried the consultant hat and gave input to planning, implementation of programs, and projects. I was like Yoda, but not getting that Hollywood recognition. Volunteer work does pay off, but make sure it aligns with your goals and career. I tried the Mommy/PTO leader hat, but while I love our school, the lack of diversity in the PTO was impactful for me.

I tried all of these hats but left my own hat on the hook because I didn't believe I was enough. When other people told me I was enough, I would look into their eyes and I wanted to run in fear. Fear is the last bridge you want to cross.

As Latinas or Chicanas, we are taught to give to our *familia*, to our husbands, and to our children. I still get teary when I leave my house, husband, and kids behind. I somehow shake off that old Mexican hat for this Wisconsin *Mujer* hat, which is who I am. The Wisconsin woman who spends her days discovering her boundaries, anchoring her goals on firm ground. In my vulnerable moments, I discovered my brand was a Mexican export, but cultivated with a Midwest point of view for outreach, marketing, and social media strategies that come from a unique place of resilience, radical self-love, and cultural awareness. As Gloria E. Anzaldúa says, "A woman who writes has power, and a woman with power is feared."

Wisconsin Mujer is a brand that helps businesses navigate diversity, much like how I have navigated through restoring myself, and I now help others do it well.

I leave you with this, follow *mujeres* who see the horizon of the ills of our society, who are working daily to undo the historical oppressions that we face in the U.S. Don't dismiss mujeres who are every day, salt of the earth, women; you can learn so much from their commitments to their families or communities.

No one will tell you how to do your business, and there is no magic, quick way to get ahead. It takes work, both inner and outer work. Focus on your message, what you want for yourself and exactly who is your audience. There will be bad days, but remember you are not alone.

BIOGRAPHY

Araceli Esparza is the founder and owner of Wisconsin Mujer, a digital media company that specializes in strategic outreach targeting diverse populations. Her experience in sales comes from ten years of working in outreach and fundraising positions with local government, colleges and large nonprofit agencies. Wisconsin Mujer has been featured in *Wisconsin Life* and Araceli is a speaker at regional conferences and workshops.

BE THE HERO IN YOUR LIFE STORY

LUIS FARIAS

"You are enough for the world you face today, so do the world a favor and be the hero in your life story."

Last year, I started going to the gym with my son while he was home from college and I thoroughly enjoyed the time we spent working out and talking about life. During the first week, I remembered just how much I had enjoyed lifting weights back in high school.

It did not take long for me to take up leg pressing, one of my favorite routines. I remember lifting 700 pounds my senior year, so I decided to push past 1,000 pounds this time around to prove to myself that age is just a number. In 2019, that target "seemed" impossible, but I subsequently hit one milestone at 1,080 pounds, and then another at 1,200 pounds.

These achievements made me realize the importance of constantly removing obstacles that block our progress and limit our potential. Too often, we stop listening to the little voice that tells us we can do anything and, tragically, put limits on our lives that were never meant to be there.

During one workout session, I decided to create a wearable reminder that anything can be achieved as long as we put in the work. My "Target Your Impossible and Make it Possible" brand serves as a reminder that nothing is impossible. There are no excuses, only possibilities to how you become the best version of yourself in and out of the gym.

I was reminded of the importance of sharing this message with others following a conversation I had with a young driver. I asked him about his job and whether he was going to school. He told me that he had taken some classes but did not finish because "he wasn't smart enough."

I stopped him on the spot and told him never to say that about himself. I recall telling him that he was smart enough to do whatever he wanted but he had to find his passion and commit to it. As someone who was not always a good writer, I can vouch for the importance of sticking with something, especially if you do not think you are good enough. If you do anything enough times, you will become an expert.

You are enough for the world you face today, so do the world a favor and be the hero in your life story. Many look to the outside for heroes when they should be looking inwardly. Know your value, know what you want out of life and pursue the things you care about relentlessly. There is absolutely nothing that you cannot accomplish with hard work, effort, faith, determination, and discipline.

Never give up just because things are not turning out the way you expect. When life knocks you down, I challenge you to not stay down. Get back up and fight for what you want. When you do this, you will make the biggest contributions in your life.

BIOGRAPHY

Luis Farias served the people of California for close to a decade prior to joining the private sector, where he guided CKE (Carl's Jr. & Hardee's) and its franchisees in navigating government. A champion of Hispanic businesses, Farias then joined a group to advocate for pro-small business policies that would facilitate growth and expansion.

Now, he works on projects to connect companies with the growing Latino population which is nearly 61 million strong and whose buying power will soon reach $2 trillion. A believer in fitness, he also launched a motivational apparel brand last year. He writes frequently about current topics.

BELIEVE IN YOUR INFINITY POWER

DALEXA FERNANDEZ

"Believe in the power of your heart!"

I was born when my mother was only 19 years old. She was a secretary and my dad was a general laborer. I grew up in a home with financial struggles in a lower middle-class neighborhood in the small town of Guanare, Venezuela. At a very young age, I could feel something inside of me that said, "You are greater than any circumstance." Yet the very place where I was born and raised helped determine my future.

When I was nine years old, we did a project about oil in my class. That was the beginning of my leadership story. In Venezuela, people often thought of oil engineers as "free people" who would travel and make a lot of money. As a young girl, I decided at that moment, to become a petroleum engineer.

Throughout my childhood, I never stopped thinking about having a radically different life than the one I thought was already chosen for me. My goal was to study and I was determined to accomplish my goal. When I was 17, I moved to Maracaibo to attend the University of Zulia. It was about six hours away from my hometown, but I was not going to let that stop me. Inside, I was powerfully determined and eager to show that my dreams were possible, and there was a world full of possibilities waiting for me.

At 22, I started working with PDVSA (Petróleos de Venezuela, S.A.), the most important oil company in Venezuela. The day I held my engineering diploma in my hands, I confirmed that dreams can come true and I felt happiness throughout my body. I felt powerful.

A few years later when I was 24, I received a job offer in Mexico, which would be a turning point in my professional life. I accepted and started working as a consultant. My desire to continue growing was just as strong, so I decided to complete a master's degree in the U.S.

My first giant challenge was to learn English. Two years later, I moved to Houston, Texas, and started English classes at the University of Houston. It was a very frustrating semester as I met the challenges of being unable to communicate in a foreign language.

Once I was fluent in English, I started my MBA. I managed to study and work as a project manager. During that time, my responsibility was to plan and execute high level oil operations. Even though it was very challenging, I was able to do it all! Today, I am a Venezuelan woman who achieved her dream to finish her MBA in Houston, the oil capital of the world.

My story has helped me to grow and to show how everything is possible, and that if I could conquer the dreams of my heart, so can you. There is nothing impossible for you because there is an infinite power that lives inside of you. I believe in my infinite power. Believe in the power of your heart!

BIOGRAPHY

Dalexa Fernandez is a transformational leader. Her "My Infinity Power" methodology integrates her 13 years of international experience in the oil and gas corporate world with her purpose in life to inspire women to accomplish their goals and objectives by connecting with the power of their hearts.

She is a petroleum engineer with an MBA, a leadership coach, and mentor. She is a Hispanic Star leader in Houston and a member of John Maxwell's team.

THE STRONGEST ABUELITAS

HECTOR FERNANDEZ

"There is no easy way."

2020 has been a challenging year for all of us and in my own personal time I've been reflecting on my executive journey and the largest influences so far. Two that are always with me are my two grandmas: one Mexican, *"Mamati"*, and the other one Guatemalan, *"Mamanina"*.

While I spent most of my time away from them since we immigrated to the U.S. when I was young, they both imparted many lessons. One of them has stayed with me during my corporate life: from investing, to investment banking and corporate finance, to most recently becoming president of a business.

I can best sum it up as, "There is no easy way."

First, as an elementary school teacher, my Mamanina dedicated her life to teaching kids in civil war-torn Quiche, Guatemala, a region that required her to walk many kilometers up and down the mountains each morning and evening. Having been left by her husband, she had to struggle on her own to educate and provide for her two boys, one of which is my father. I routinely have thought of her strength of will and perseverance, not only in becoming the first MBA in my family, but in building our own family here in the U.S.

For Mamati, she was born in Mexico but adopted Guatemala and devoted her life to educating the young, co-founding a K-12 school in Guatemala City in 1954. For her and my paternal grandfather, it was a life-long mission of investing days, nights, and weekends, trying to build a now 65-year-old educational institution that would impact kid's hearts and minds.

Neither of them had many weekends off, vacations in far-away places, nor the ability to take time later in life for their own advanced education, but these are all great opportunities and blessings that have come to me here in the U.S. Instead, they both had to face significant challenges from being women that wanted to push boundaries in a society that many times were not ready or accommodating toward strong women with even stronger ambitions. Even so, I will always remember this--they did not complain nor accuse others regarding their circumstances. Instead, they both focused on doing daily what they could without worrying about what society or challenges came their way.

And so it was that as I went back to Guatemala during my high school years to spend summers with our family, I'd hear these stories of the "old days" – peppered with their humor and sometimes with tears--of what it was like to get up day after day chasing their own missions in life, not waiting for it to come to them, and not expecting that it'd be easy. In fact, there was, and is no easy way.

So, as 2020 challenges come and go, that's what I'm hoping to teach my own kids – put in the work and focus on what you can control – just like the *abuelitas* taught us.

BIOGRAPHY

Hector Fernandez was born in Guatemala City, Guatemala, and immigrated to Miami, Florida, with his family in the 1990s. Before completing his MBA at Northwestern's Kellogg School of Management, he worked in investment management. He worked in New York City for J.P. Morgan in their technology, media, and telecom investment banking group and later in the Harris Williams Consumer & Food group.

Hector joined Cargill in 2013 and founded Cargill's Corporate Financial Planning & Analysis (FP&A) group as well as taking on divisional CFO responsibilities. From 2018-2020 he served as president of Cargill Risk Management and in prior years was chair of the Cargill Hispanic & Latino Council.

WHAT DOESN'T KILL YOU MAKES YOU STRONGER

KATERYN FERREIRA

"Action is the foundational key to success."

Growing up for me was loaded with all sorts of trauma, including my parent's divorce, being raised by a single young mother, childhood adversity, and bullying. Despite all these circumstances, I became a resilient Latina. As you read this, I am overcoming all this so-called "baggage" and putting all those excuses and limitations aside.

All these adversities have not only made me the person I am today, but they have strengthened my courage, driving me to excel in my aspirations. This independence and drive have helped me to conquer without seeking the approval of others. If you want to do something, DO IT!

As a young Hispanic and first-generation American, I want to empower and inspire future generations who are struggling with shortcomings, insecurities, and mind-created barriers that inhibit them from accomplishing what they want. Everybody's story is different, and we Hispanics are authentic, strong, passionate, resilient, and unstoppable.

I've had the honor to meet very inspirational Hispanics who have pushed me to excel. They have created an empire of their own, but they have struggled to get there. It is also important to highlight our accomplishments, for they are the fuel that keeps us pushing for more and creating that fire. Action is the foundational key to success.

I can proudly say that I excelled throughout my education and career. I completed my Bachelor of Science in health services administration with *magna cum laude* honors. My struggles have really humbled me to be a passionate, loving, and compassionate person.

I love to help others and give back to my community. As a public health advocate, a Hispanic leader, and female warrior, I continue to conquer my passion to help others by empowering, educating, and inspiring.

Nothing is easy in life. You just need courage to get started and keep pushing. If you have courage, you can accomplish anything. Obstacles don't kill you, they make you stronger. I have learned that at a very young age.

My life has taught me many lessons, and I believe that the limit of your success and happiness is in your mind. If I am doing it, you could do the same. What is stopping you? Those limitations are in your head.

We Hispanics and Latinos have heritage, beliefs, backgrounds, and struggles that follow through the generations. Many of us have immigrated to the United States to make a better life for our families. Sometimes those values and beliefs keep us from expecting and asking for more. Stand up as the Hispanic you are!

BIOGRAPHY

Kateryn Ferreira is Dominican, born and raised in Washington Heights. She currently works for NYC Health and Hospitals as a Community Engagement Supervisor, advocating for the COVID Test and Trace Initiative.

She worked at Montefiore Medical Center located in the Bronx for more than six years, employing her talents in customer service, community outreach, and program management. She also owns businesses in direct marketing as an independent consultant for Touchstone Crystal by Swarovski, Farmasi, and Pure Romance.

Kateryn received her education at the City University of New York (CUNY) School of Public Health and earned a master's degree in public health in community health education. She also holds a bachelor's degree in health service administration from CUNY Lehman College.

WRITE YOUR OWN STORY

JANIE FLORES

"If I had waited for the invitations to have a seat at the table, receive invitations for speaking engagements, or for doors to magically open, I would not have accomplished anything."

I always enter a room with a smile on my face and an air of confidence and authority, whether I feel it or not. The confidence is born from a sense of purpose and from the lessons of faith and integrity that my parents instilled into my life. They never doubted that I was destined to do great things. It took many years and overcoming many obstacles for me to fully believe that, but every day I would step out and take actions that would bring me closer to believing their words.

My passion has always been to serve and empower people with the abilities and gifts I possess. Giving back to my community, wherever I have lived, has been a practice from early on. I was the youngest commissioner appointed to the housing authority and served as vice president of the board for the first community health center in my hometown in southeastern Wisconsin, all while working to support my son as a single parent in low wage jobs.

Years later, when I left a comfortable corporate position to launch my company, Buena Vida Media, I ensured that part of the culture of the company was serving the community in South Florida. As a new entrepreneur, I quickly learned that I had to forge a path for myself in a very competitive market. People who were friends when I worked for the large, well-known corporation were not opening doors and giving me a seat at the table as a solopreneur. I had to make the decision to forego the feelings of self-pity and instead, I decided to write my own story.

If I had waited for the invitations to have a seat at the table, receive invitations for speaking engagements, or for doors to magically open, I would not have accomplished anything. The rejections propelled me to create and produce conferences where I give lesser known voices the opportunity to be presenters, to create and produce television, radio, and podcast shows where I highlight the positive contributions made by the multicultural community in this country. As a result of those experiences and lessons, my business has grown beyond a multimedia company and has expanded to include coaching entrepreneurs to execute in the face of obstacles, fears, and insecurities.

We are living in unparalleled times. To whom much is given, much is required. Those same abilities and gifts that made room for me in the entrepreneurial world now have to be used in service to my community, locally and nationally.

The COVID-19 pandemic is wreaking havoc and

disproportionately affecting the Latino community. At the same time, the fight for racial and social justice on behalf of our Brown and Black brothers and sisters has intensified. We must proactively take action to serve, contribute, or lead. We must write our own story and determine the legacy we want to leave for future generations.

BIOGRAPHY

Janie Flores, President of Buena Vida Media, harnesses the power of the media to catapult her clients to success by strategically using promotions, productions and publicity to position them in the market.

Janie produces and hosts *Janie Flores Live*, a radio and podcast show highlighting the positive contributions made by the multicultural community in the U.S., airing every Friday on 880TheBiz.com, the only Bloomberg News affiliate in South Florida.

Janie is a Hispanic Women of Distinction Honoree 2020, a 100 Successful Women in Business honoree, a Premio a la Excelencia - Galapagos Islands, Ecuador, honoree, among other recognitions.

CINTHIA N. FLORES

"I was experiencing the purest form of self-hate."

As a teenager, my aunt recruited me to work weekends with her as a house cleaning helper. I accepted her offer because I felt the need to become financially independent to alleviate a bit of the economic pressure on my single mom, who worked in the Los Angeles garment industry to maintain a household of five.

I performed the "easy tasks," which included sweeping, mopping, and washing dishes. More importantly, I served as my aunt's personal interpreter and communicated with her white employers on her behalf. My aunt is a monolingual Spanish speaker.

I remember my aunt became smaller in the room when her employer and I spoke English. At first, I was relieved that my aunt's invisibility distinguished us in the eyes of her employers. It was as if my ability to speak English reflected my "American identity." Over time, however, I recognized how painful this experience was for both of us. I realized that the English language became a marker of distinction between her and I – an indication of both the celebration of acculturation and vilification of "foreigners."

After about three years of working with my aunt, I accepted a weekend job with a telemarketing agency. When I informed my aunt that I would no longer accompany her to clean houses, she turned to me and said, "Now that you've got an office job, you're not going to want to associate with people like your mother and me." In that moment, I comprehended the significance of my actions--my aunt was also painfully aware of the division the English language had created between us.

How could I, someone that grew up in the same household and enjoyed spending time with family, take comfort in my aunt's invisibility? Easy. I was experiencing the purest form of self-hate. The kind of self-hate that motivates us to create as much distance between ourselves and those parts of our lived experiences that mainstream society deems unworthy of acceptance.

Upon this realization, I underwent a great awakening. I invested much energy in understanding the delicate relationship between acculturation and otherness, ultimately arriving at the truth that claiming my place in "American" society did not have to come at the expense of others.

Over the years, I have referenced this moment as a central part of my development. I am grateful to my aunt for providing me with the opportunity to work alongside her and learn a very valuable lesson, how to exist as an authentic person in a country that sought to erase my lived experience to project an image of an equal society. This experience also inculcated the importance of honoring the dignified labor of working people from all backgrounds. Equally as important, it facilitated my commitment to creating a just society for all.

BIOGRAPHY

Cinthia Flores is a board member of the California Agricultural Labor Relations Board. Currently, Cinthia serves on the board for Latinas Lead California, a political action committee dedicated to electing Latinas. She also serves on the Latina Lawyers Bar Association, a nonprofit organization dedicated to supporting Latinas in the legal profession.

Cinthia serves on the UCLA Alumni Association and is a graduate of the University of California, Irvine School of Law. During law school, Cinthia served as a regent on the University of California Board of Regents. She is also a graduate of UCLA. While at UCLA, she served as the first Latina student body president.

KEEP KNOCKING AND THE DOOR WILL BE OPENED

ARTHUR GARCIA

"Rent was due, so I had to keep knocking."

I was hungry and alone on a rainy February day in San Francisco's Mission District in 2006. I was wearing my only suit, it was wet, I had knocked on 78 doors, and had only one sale and 77 rejections that ranged from "no soliciting" to "I'm calling security."

I was a first-generation recent college graduate in a new city, and full of pride as the first in the family to leave home. I was a door-to-door paper salesman, working in a 100 percent-commission multi-level marketing opportunity. Sales is a numbers game, and I knew that 90-100 door knocks would get me to 10 decision makers and make two or three sales per day.

I was motivated, and a hunter. If I didn't sell, I didn't eat, and I wanted so badly to make my family proud by selling enough to open my own office.

My parents were my model. They owned their own restaurant, and to me, entrepreneurship was success. It was raining and I wanted to go home, but rent was due, so I had to keep knocking. I had 22 doors to go and only a few more doors slammed in my face. Door number 92 was an accounting firm that purchased 10 cases of paper. Finally, a sale!

I grew up in Commerce City, Colorado, an industrial community northeast of Denver and home to the Suncor oil refinery, the Mile High dog track, and the Rocky Mountain Arsenal, a former chemical weapons factory during WWII.

I wasn't supposed to make it out. My high school had the highest dropout rate in the state and teen pregnancy was so bad that daycare was provided on campus. The college counselor told me to pick another major due to an insufficient GPA for the business school.

I refused to give up and found a way to accomplish my goal by committing to my academics and after five years, I did it. I graduated with a B.S. in business, two minors, and a certificate in ethnic studies. I kept on knocking and did not give up.

After receiving a rejection letter from graduate school on a Friday in 2008, and praying for direction over that weekend, an email came the following Thursday that the letter I received was an error. Two years later, I received the first master's degree in the family.

I am thankful for every opportunity I have had to learn and believe each challenge has prepared me for the next breakthrough. Selling paper made me a stronger sales professional.

My MBA and management experience opened the door for a leadership role at a tech company focused on small businesses and accountants. I was recognized in the Top 20 under 40 in the accounting industry recognition in 2018. The following year I was leading a national tax franchise and made *Entrepreneur Magazine's* top 500 list of franchises.

I could have stayed home to run the restaurant, picked another major, or gone home because it was raining, but instead I kept knocking.

BIOGRAPHY

Arthur Garcia is a business executive, consult and community builder. As a marketing and sales leader, he has helped thousands of businesses add efficiencies through technology, processes, and talent.

He is co-founder of the Contabi Alliance, a professional accounting community that delivers advisory across borders. He consults in the fintech and service industry.

Arthur is a graduate of Colorado State University, the University of San Francisco, and the Stanford Latino Entrepreneurship Initiative (SLEI) Scaling Program.

STREET SIDE FREEDOM

JENNIFER GARCIA

"There is such freedom when you release the opinions of others."

I grew up in a small town often described as, "so small if you blink, you'll miss it." Life in Mora, New Mexico, was simple. We had dirt roads, no streetlights, one school, and our nearest neighbor was 300 yards up the road.

Rural living also meant that the majority of the community was self-employed, as was the case for my father. During my formative years, he sold what he could to support our family. For years we would dig small trees and wrap them in burlap, gather truckloads of firewood, pick rock and boulders, and then drive to a nearby city and sit on the side of the road to sell. As I grew older, I was embarrassed to be seen on the side of the road.

I was trapped by the opinions of others.

My mom was an educator, but also did what she could to support the family. Every year for Mother's Day she would order 3,000 roses and resell them in our community. I would dethorn

3,000 roses and wrap them in bouquets. If that wasn't painful enough, I would then knock on each classroom door selling roses to students. We then parked on the side of the street in the "vendor corner" of our small town and sold roses to the community. With age and greater awareness of peer perception, the more I dreaded Mother's Day weekend.

I was still trapped by the opinions of others.

After college, I got a corporate job in San Francisco. The first time my mother came to visit, I took her to my office on the 35th floor of a high rise in the financial district. I was confused by her tears running down her face as she toured my office building. I can still hear the shakiness of her voice as she said "Jenn, you've come so far." City living, skyscrapers, subways, an amazing job with a 360-degree view of San Francisco, was so distant from my roots in Mora, New Mexico.

I worked in finance and with an amazing company for over a decade. I frequently received accolades for my career; a lucrative job with all the right benefits, but inside my heart longed for more. If I had stopped there, I would have been deemed a success story.

Over time I realized that I was trapped by golden handcuffs.

Two years ago, I resigned and launched my own company. I traded a lucrative job for zero income. I effectively went back to sitting on the side of the road, selling to provide for my family. As I reflect on the hustle of parents and my very own hustle, I realize that there is such freedom when you release the opinions of others.

I am learning that I can do the ugly, the unpopular, the embarrassing, and I can pursue my dream, with freedom. And that alone is success.

BIOGRAPHY

Jennifer Garcia is a business and leadership consultant and is committed to helping businesses grow and equipping leaders to elevate their potential. She has over 14 years of experience in the fintech industry, with extensive experience in sales, product development, customer support, and leadership.

She also directs the Scaling Program for Latino Business Action Network in collaboration with Stanford University to equip Latino/a business owners to scale their business; with the goal of increasing the number of scaled Latino-owned businesses in the United States.

Jennifer received her bachelor's degree at Colorado State University and obtained her MBA at the University of San Francisco. She is a certified coach through The John Maxwell Team.

BLOOD, SWEAT, AND BERTHA

JESSIE GARCIA

"Building a company is an endurance game, not a sprint. Tomorrow is always a new day, and oftentimes you're better off starting fresh than pushing through."

It was July 3, 2018, and everyone was shuffling out of our co-working space to head out to the Jersey Shore for the Fourth of July. I called my fiancé Chris and told him I was staying late. I knew he was disappointed, but he supported me and reminded me to be safe and have our engineer, Tom, stay with me to help. We had an upcoming delivery and there was no way I was going to let a little holiday throw off our timeline. I didn't want to disappoint our customer.

I fired up Bertha, our 1978, 15-ton plastic-injection molding machine. I prepped the plastic pellets and molds like I had done hundreds of times before. Every 30-second cycle, Bertha's steel mouth opened and closed pushing out more and more plastic parts. Bertha was the embodiment of Tozuda's journey; scrappy, hardworking, and yet unpredictable.

Back in 2016, when we were just starting our product development, I remember getting quotes back from manufacturers for $50K, sometimes even more, to have them make our product. As a bootstrapped entrepreneur, those quotes nearly took the life out of the company and built a barrier I thought would be impossible to overcome.

Instead, we forged our own path forward. We found this old, broken machine on Ebay for $1,000 dollars, and spent nearly six months refurbishing her to get her up and running, with only an instruction manual in German to guide us.

Our team worked tirelessly learning how to design injection molds, operate computer numerical control (CNC) machines to make them, and fine tune the process to get crystal clear plastic parts. We became a manufacturing company out of necessity and no quote was going to stop us from making our vision a reality.

After a couple of hours of sweating and operating Bertha that humid night in July, a part got clogged in the machine. As I reached down into the mold to clear it, I pressed the wrong button just for a second, and 15-tons of force closed on my right hand. The damage from Bertha's bite was immediate.

As I bled and Tom rushed me to the hospital, I thought every bone was crushed and that I had lost my hand. Thankfully, I just needed lots of stitches and several months of rehab to get full functionality back. When letting the customer know the delivery would be delayed after all, we were met with empathy and understanding, instead of disappointment.

Without your health, you don't have anything. I did more damage that one night because I was nervous about taking just one day off. Building a company is an endurance game, not a sprint.

Tomorrow is always a new day, and oftentimes you're better off starting fresh than pushing through. I got my strong work ethic and creativity from my Cuban family and I will keep forging Tozuda's path forward, no matter what, but you can believe that I now take July 3 and July 4 off.

BIOGRAPHY

Jessie Garcia is the founder and CEO of Tozuda, a sports and industrial safety product manufacturing company based in Philadelphia. She is a patented inventor, and her core mechanical acceleration technology is now an award-winning, affordable device that helps users know when they have sustained a damaging head impact. All you have to remember is, "If it's RED, check your head. ™"

Using her personal experiences with concussions, she is determined to make safety assessments simpler and more affordable to everyone. Jessie is a proud Lehigh University graduate with a master's degree in engineering and is also a Stanford Latino Entrepreneurship Leadership Fellow.

FROM INVISIBLE TO INVINCIBLE

SAMÍ HAIMAN-MARRERO

Samí Haiman-Marrero

"Hispanics are not invisible. We are invincible."

When I was eight, my Nuyorican parents moved our family from New York to rural Puerto Rico. I didn't speak Spanish and was labeled "la gringa" at the public school stationed between a dirt road and a coffee plantation.

Eventually, the community of Barrio Frontón acknowledged me as a fellow Boricua. My parents advocated for just causes on the island, dragging us kids to every march held in San Juan. I hated it, but their activism instilled in me a strong commitment to community.

After college, I returned to the U.S. in pursuit of career success. With a master's degree, full command of English, and the naïveté of youth, I thought I was the "dopest" girl on earth. Nothing could stop me. My plans received a reality check in the world of magazine publishing. As I swam in a sea of white men who labeled me as a working-class Hispanic female, I was basically invisible, and it pissed me off.

Working on Hispanic publications inside big media, I absorbed tons of knowledge about the "burgeoning Latino segment" to be able to claim it as my expertise. I thought it might be valuable someday. I developed a special sisterhood with other Latina professionals experiencing the same challenges.

Sandra from Perú, Marcia from Ecuador, Roxana from Argentina, Laura from Mexico, and many more were also overlooked, overworked, and underpaid. Nothing has changed. A 2012 American Association of University Women study revealed that Hispanic women earn on average 53 cents for each dollar earned by white males doing the same work.

I found a mentor. My boss, a woke white woman, taught me to navigate the prejudices of white men. "Keep your eye on the bottom-line," "Be precise and concise," "Analyze data," "Speak up," "Set boundaries," "Ignore their comments," she advised.

Every U.S. Census becomes a wake-up call for America about the impact of Hispanics on the nation's future. In 2000, I became an asset to company leadership, the in-house expert regarding the "burgeoning Latino segment." It happened! But it came with a price.

I experienced the ugly: stereotyping, back-stabbing, verbal attacks, unwanted advances, and unequal pay. However, I realized I wasn't invisible anymore. I was now an armadillo: thick-skinned, long-clawed, with a keen sense of smell–much needed weaponry to combat the bullshit I was dealing with.

I lost my job in 2018 to the recession. Almost 40, I asked, "What are my chances of landing a job in a sea of unemployed people, including white males?" I decided to join the millions of Hispanic entrepreneurs fueling this country's economy, finding my voice once stifled by a system that wanted to define me.

America had another wake-up call after the 2010 Census. As experts in the burgeoning Latino segment, we segued into diversity and inclusion and onboarding clients who understood the importance of equity and cultural competency.

Hispanics are not invisible. We are invincible. Today, we are committed to purposeful work and creating inclusive environments where everyone can thrive–on my terms, as a Hispanic businesswoman, and an activist.

BIOGRAPHY

Samí Haiman-Marrero is the president/CEO of Urbander, a Minority and Women Business Enterprise (MWBE) that assists the corporate, nonprofit, and government sectors overcome their diversity, equity, inclusion, and multicultural marketing challenges.

PLAYING FULL OUT!

IVONNE E. HANKS

"Stop twiddling your thumbs. You are the eureka moment you are waiting for! Be presence itself!"

I can share so many personal anecdotes that have shaped me into the person that I am, but this one in particular best conveys my awakening to enlightenment, and to a life of community service.

In the late 90s, I was wandering the streets of New York City aimlessly, until a sign caught my attention. It read, "Sixteen miles of books inside. The Strand bookstore." With my love for books, I was lured immediately. Of course, I had to go see this for myself!

I perused the store, looking at all the different books. As I ventured to the back of the store, my eyes landed on an orange book all the way on the top row close to the high ceiling. Out of curiosity, I asked the attendant why the orange book was among all the dark-colored books.

He responded, "Actually, that book doesn't belong in the rare books section. I will go get the ladder." He handed me the book, *The*

Teachings of Buddha. I felt an instant connection with the rhythm of the language that resonated to my spirit.

Unbeknownst to me, this book began awakening me to a life of consciousness, discerning life's synchronicities, such as this one! You see, when we are fully conscious of the present moment, we are able to recognize all the synchronicities. Perhaps you think of them as coincidences, but they are not. Nothing in life happens by chance!

You see, synchronicities are a series of events that the universe arranges itself in response to our heart's desires and the thoughts that we are creating in our minds in guiding us to our life purpose.

The wisdom that I received from it led me to cultivate a life of consciousness every day. "Living in the Spirit" with childlike wonder, joy, and awe. I learned that in the human condition we operate from two states of being: a conscious state or an unconscious state. That one state is suffering, and the other, free of suffering.

It taught me that all suffering originates from the unconscious state of being, driven by all kinds of life dissatisfactions, that have not been fulfilled. And, that from these two states, we choose how to respond to life experiences.

When I am being present, my spirit feels free of suffering and connected to all there is. I allow my intuition to guide me with the intelligence to overcome all life's adversities. In this state of being, I am able to co-create the life of my heart's desires.

To me, this book revealed the greatest mystery to mankind, hidden underneath our nose, which is that we are our own imagination, as the image and liking of the Divine. We create the life that we think and only by being present can we harness our heart's intelligence and desires. So, stop twiddling your thumbs. You are the eureka moment you are waiting for! Be presence itself!

BIOGRAPHY

Ivonne Hanks is an author, an international speaker, and a mindfulness advocate. With a career in health and human services, she encourages mindful civic engagement to make a difference in their community.

In her Health Is You practice, Ivonne offers transformative health and wellness life skills, and guidance for a purpose driven life of significance. She is the founder of Worldwide Culture-Link, a social-marketing, multicultural, and mindful leadership strategic communications consulting firm.

Today, Ivonne travels the world speaking and inspiring transformative and mindful leadership.

DIANA IRACHETA

"I want to change how STEM and engineering are perceived by young people."

All my life, I have faced a multitude of stereotypes. I like to think of my situation as the accumulation of as many minority categories thrown together. However, through my life, I have learned that my future does not depend on what others say or how they catalog me. I get to decide who and what I want to be. So, I decided to be everything you wouldn't expect. I am a female. I am an immigrant. I am a Latina. I am an engineer.

Think about how women can say they are all of these things. Not many. And I am here to change that.

I went into engineering school knowing that it would be a challenge. I was scared every second of it. Not only were the classes difficult, but I was also in a place where I was the complete opposite of my classmates. I had a couple challenges to overcome. For example, the first exams of every semester were the worst. I would end up with really low grades only a couple weeks into the semester. It would make me rethink my decisions and ability to continue on my journey. I obviously didn't fit in, and I wasn't doing very well either.

I am glad I decided to stay. Every time I felt scared or unsure, I had to remind myself that it was okay, as long as it didn't stop me from working towards my goals. As the semesters passed and I advanced in my studies, my grades would improve as well. I went from being a C student and failing classes, to becoming a straight-A student by graduation. My confidence increased; I knew I was in the right place, and I became an engineer.

Becoming an engineer was one of my many goals, but I knew I wouldn't encounter many others like myself. Now that I am able to say that I am an *ingeniera*, I want to continue making a change. I want to change how STEM and engineering are perceived by young people. I created a brand that focuses on empowering women in STEM, especially Latinas in engineering.

My biggest mission is to demonstrate the incredible work behind engineering and to show that anyone can be an engineer. I want to break the stereotypes. My brand's theme is pink, the color that someone is least likely to associate with engineering. That is why I picked it. Because we are in an era where engineering is for everyone, but also because the way I look, dress, or the things I like, do not make me less of an engineer.

BIOGRAPHY

Diana Iracheta is a first-generation Mexican immigrant. She is a mechanical and manufacturing engineer and the founder of "Latina Engineer," a blog, Instagram account, YouTube channel, and online shop.

There, she shares her experiences as a minority in engineering and creates educational content for STEM students.

GETTING OUT OF YOUR COMFORT ZONE AND FOLLOWING YOUR PASSION

ENNA JIMENEZ

"If you're handed it, you can handle it."

The subject read: "It's not a goodbye, it's a see you later." I stared at a blank page, then started writing, "During the last six years here, I have met some very wonderful people, created friendships that will last a lifetime, shared many laughs and stories (danced the night away at the holiday parties!), and most of all enjoyed working with a great group of colleagues. I have a picture frame on my cube which reads: 'If you're handed it, you can handle it.' That totally describes my experience here."

I read this a few times, wiped the tears from my eyes and sent the email. It was the hardest decision in my career. I loved this company, my friends and colleagues, and most importantly, I believed in the mission. I made the decision to leave a place that gave me so much because I had achieved more than what I could have ever imagined, and it was time to find the next challenging opportunity.

Let's start from the beginning. The first few weeks at the company would shape what the next six years led me to accomplish. I can still hear my manager asking me if I had met with the managing partner at the company yet.

"Oh, I didn't even know he was a managing partner," I replied. "He is Latino, we had coffee, and had a true connection."

That first interaction with a managing partner from the business led me to be included in so many opportunities around the organization. A simple, "Hello, my name is Enna. I just joined the company, and I'm also Latina." I took a risk, and some would tell me, "That's your nature Enna, to just reach out and connect with others."

I've had the great ability to be a connector and an influencer. I figured if you're handed it, you can handle it. I worked really hard at becoming a subject matter expert in my field and applied that towards improving the company's return on investment.

I looked at everything through my quality lens–whether it was planning an employee resource group or community event or the next big product release milestone. I walked through the hallways thinking, strategizing, collaborating, creating, and implementing in all areas of my daily work.

I challenged the status quo, created opportunities for innovation, and, most importantly, led with passion. I have worked at many organizations in my career where I've had the opportunity of growth, development, and impact. I had the pleasure to combine both my passion for work and my passion for diversity and inclusion and was able to be my authentic self every day. And that was when I realized how bittersweet it was when it was time for me to say goodbye.

Was it the best decision? Absolutely. I have gained many new skills and would not be the leader I am today without having experienced the loss of what felt to me, at that time, the best company, colleagues, and friends I had ever had the pleasure to work with.

BIOGRAPHY

Enna is a senior IT and business professional with expertise in quality assurance management and team restructuring and transformation. She has a huge passion for diversity and inclusion, talent engagement, community organizations, and hopes to share her expertise with corporate boards in the future.

Most recently, the National Diversity Council selected Enna as one of the 2019 National Latino Leader Award winners and she received a citation from Governor of Massachusetts Charlie Baker on Leadership and Excellence in 2019.

Enna is a mom with four children and has four beautiful grandchildren. She is a Puerto Rican born, Dominican-raised, Bostonian who loves dancing salsa, bachata, and merengue.

ANYONE AND EVERYONE CAN CHANGE THE WORLD. IT COULD BE YOU, ME, OR US

SCARLETT LANZAS

"Seek within yourself what your purpose in life is, focus on the positive you have to give to the world and act upon it!"

I come from a place where women are considered resilient and resourceful, some might even say fearless. I was born in Nicaragua just when a civil war was fueling, and everyday life turned dangerous really quick.

My parents decided to migrate to give us a better life and a chance to get a quality education. I guess experiencing leaving everything behind and starting over many times made me embrace change. I see change as a good thing. I learned to be resilient and developed the capacity to adapt. I take on challenges as opportunities to learn new things about me and the world I live in.

Since change had always been a constant in my life, I decided early on that I wanted to change the world. I had to prepare for this journey. Thank God I had the support from my family, the drive to push myself, to pursue three degrees and fellowships to diversify my skills as the journey would not be an easy one.

Changing the world is not a simple task. I was fortunate to start my career at the United Nations World Food Programme. Working for the largest humanitarian agency in the world truly shaped me into becoming a thoughtful and compassionate professional, it was the best school of life.

Years later, life took me to New Orleans, where I was starting over. I had to adapt since my professional experience was in international development and humanitarian assistance. New Orleans was a complex place to live and work. It is a city full of colors and music, its food is unique, and its people are so loving. However, New Orleans is a city with deep economic inequities and racial tensions.

Fate and an urgent sense to serve the Latino community led me to take the role of executive director at the only Latino-serving organization. At times I felt uncertain about taking on so many issues--immigration reform, advocating for language access in schools, open governance, health disparities, and economic inequality.

I had to reinvent myself and find creative ways to use my talents and experience to embrace community development, policy, and advocacy work. I reached out to thoughtful leaders that supported me in my mission to work with and for Latinos.

I'm particularly proud of the work we did with Dreamers (recipients of the Deferred Action for Childhood Arrivals-DACA). We provided leadership development programs and connected our youth to scholarships and higher education resources. We cried tears of joy when DACA was signed. That was a life-changing and special day for all Dreamers around the country.

Our Latino youth leaders are now all grown up, have great jobs, are creating positive social change, and making amazing contributions in their communities. Just two weeks ago, one of them reached out and said, "Y'all were amazing role models. I remember being in admiration of the work y'all were doing." That made my worries and hard work in New Orleans all worth it.

It's important to seek within yourself what your purpose in life is, focus on the positive you have to give to the world and act upon it. If you can change one life, you are changing the world for that person!

BIOGRAPHY

Scarlett Lanzas is a social entrepreneur with a demonstrated history of working with public and private sector agencies, nonprofits, and international development and humanitarian assistance organizations.

As an impact investor, in her current role as chief community officer at Emergent Global Investments, she focuses on the strategic design of investment products and services related to impact investing by combining her passion for the United Nations Sustainable Development Goals Framework with environmental, social and governance investment criteria.

She co-founded Social Impact Movement and is a Hispanic Star Ambassador. Scarlett holds an executive Master of Public Administration degree from Florida International University.

MAKING MY OWN PATH

ESTHER LEDESMA PUMAROL

"I lived through the words 'representation matters' and how critical it is to be yourself wherever you go."

"You can't take those *maletas*, you have to leave one," said the airline representative.

It was an increasingly warm day that December. It was past midnight and I could feel the humidity from the Caribbean Sea right outside the airport in Santo Domingo, D.R. That night, I was taking a one-way flight to New York City at two o'clock in the morning.

At 22 years old, my life, career, and dreams were packed in those two pieces of luggage. They were carefully weighed and ready to board a plane that would leave behind my life as I knew it. Hearing her words meant an inconsolable moment of disruption and change, something very familiar to me that I had to embrace early in life.

Growing up in a *barrio* on the west side of Santo Domingo, I was familiar with living in a small, rented apartment and walking everywhere. It felt no different going to stay with my family in New Jersey. I had no job, no plan, and many dreams to pursue. I remember feeling this fire inside me, pushing me to keep going.

Since middle school and growing up seeing my mom working as a teacher, the importance of education was clear to me very early in life. When I made it to high school, I quickly learned I had to work hard if I wanted to obtain a college degree and pursue a career, which meant developing an internal mission to overcome systemic barriers and challenging my surroundings at the time. That fire continues to burn inside me, and fuels me even today.

It only took me 30 days to find a job and move to Massachusetts. That meant moving to a different state, with no home, no plan, and a friend of a friend who welcomed me. We Dominicans are known for being friendly, and that warmth helped me make it through the year I lived there. I learned many lessons and faced challenges while working as the only minority and female engineer onsite.

Many times, I had to prove myself professionally, especially as the only one in the room that looked like me. However, I'm a self-starter, a trailblazer, and I had a mission to succeed and grow.

A year later, I decided to change roles, which meant moving again. This was one of the key decisions that was responsible for progressing my career and getting me where I am today. After accepting a new role and moving down to South Carolina, I started to recognize the value of taking risks and owning my path.

Fast forward to 2020 and I've lived in five states, had

multiple professional experiences, managed a career change, and taken a strong role of advocacy for minorities and the importance of diversity in the workplace. I've lived through the words "representation matters," and how critical it is to be yourself wherever you go.

I am a proud Latina and will continue to channel that fire that burns inside me, motivating me to keep going and inspire all those coming after me.

BIOGRAPHY

Esther Ledesma Pumarol is originally from Santo Domingo, DR. She's a global portfolio marketing manager at Medtronic. She has held several engineering and marketing roles across the U.S. and is a graduate from Instituto Tecnologico de Santo Domingo with a bachelor's degree in industrial and product design.

She has a M.S. in new product development from Rochester Institute of Technology, and an MBA with an emphasis in international business and marketing from the University of Wisconsin.

Esther serves as the president for the Society of Hispanic Professional Engineers, Twin Cities chapter, and as the co-chair for the Hispanic Latino Network at Medtronic. She's a co-author for the book, *"Green Card STEM Voices: Stories from Minnesota Immigrants."*

EL CAPITAN

ROY LOVE

"Todo se puede!"

"Todo se puede." Everything is doable. That's what my junior high teacher told me once. I have never forgotten. He was a great mentor and teacher. The driver behind a good student is a great teacher. Sometimes that teacher is a parent, and sometimes it is someone like Mr. Medina.

I have always dreamt of being a captain. Having fulfilled that dream, I can say that while it may seem easy, there were times I almost gave up.

I was born on an island. Most of my ancestors were merchants, and I have always been drawn to the sea. Watching waves break on the shore, taking in the salt air sitting under a palm tree, and watching ships and fishing boats on the horizon are unforgettable memories.

Moving to New York in 1983 was tough for a kid used to beaches, sand, and running free. There were no ships in the Bronx, or so I thought. Having done well in junior high, working hard and graduating as salutatorian from PS 151, I was given the opportunity to attend a brand-new high school in Queens. Mr. Medina made sure I made it there.

Today, Townsend Harris High School is one of the top schools in the U.S. I think it was my third year in high school that I first rode over the Throggs Neck Bridge and saw the Ship Empire State moored at the pier of State University of New York Maritime College.

Every time I saw that ship, I remembered my dream. I imagined myself on the bridge, sailing into the sunset. Now I had to figure out how to pay for college. Fortunately, my brother had already joined the Navy. I thought about his time at the Naval Academy, the uniforms he wore, and the stories he told.

That would be my life. I figured out that the Navy ROTC could pay for my entire four years of college. I applied for a scholarship and was accepted to SUNY. In 1989, I started at Maritime, and four years later I would walk out with a bachelor's degree and closer to my dream.

It would take 16 years of hard work to finally be selected to command a ship. I had served in many assignments before, as a division officer, department head, and executive officer. Along the way, there were times I thought I might not make it. My tours were longer than most of my classmates, and possibly more challenging, as one of only a few minorities on my ships.

I was passed over for department head the first year, because of timing. Despite performing well as a department head, I was passed over twice for XO, making it on my final look. I almost left the Navy then, out of frustration. My wife urged patience. I excelled as an XO and was selected for command at sea in 2009! I took command of my ship, the USS BOONE FFG 28, in 2010.

I smiled and cried quietly in the captain's cabin that day. Thank you, Mr. Medina, for believing in me. You were right. Todo se puede!

BIOGRAPHY

Captain Love was born in the Dominican Republic, enlisted in the Navy in 1988, and graduated from SUNY Maritime in 1993. He attended the Naval War College in Newport, Rhode Island, earning a master's in national security in 2008, then deployed to Iraq during Operation Iraqi Freedom in 2009.

He served as Commanding Officer of USS BOONE (FFG 28) in 2010, leading the ship to win the Battle Efficiency award in 2011.

In 2016, he assumed command of Naval Base San Diego, the second largest naval installation in the world, culminating his tour in 2019 after winning the Installation Excellence Award.

PERSIST TO FIND THE OPPORTUNITIES, EVEN WHEN THEY SAY NO

MAYRA A. LOZANO

"Success occurs when opportunity meets preparation."

Every parents' dream is for their kids to grow up one day and say, "Mom, dad, I want to be an actor." Yes, that was a joke. Well, imagine the look on my parent's faces when I turned down a full ride to University of California Davis to be a vet, and said yes to an acting academy in Hollywood. It was probably the same face you are making now as you read this.

Although it was an utter shock, they never cut my wings. Instead, they were incredibly supportive. Choosing to go to an acting academy turned out to be an incredibly inconvenient and difficult path. I didn't have money to pay for tuition, let alone live in LA. I had to wake up at four o'clock in the morning to drive an hour and a half commute every single day for two years.

After an intense time in the program, I graduated, only to

admit that I was not ready to call myself an actor and I needed more training. Therefore, I applied to the University of Southern California (USC) three days before the deadline. I called every day to get an audition to their dramatic arts school, but they were fully booked. Still, I found out when, where, and what time the LA auditions were being held. I arrived at a very intimidating campus and was immediately lost.

I eventually found the auditions and sat in the middle of dozens of nervous students ready to be called in. I waited many hours trying to figure out how I would get into that room if my name wasn't on the list. After many hours, there were only a few of us left. Suddenly, they called a name, and it wasn't mine. When nobody responded, they called it again. Again, no response. They called it for a third time, and my feet stood me up without my permission.

I walked straight into the room, shut the door, and immediately blurted out my real name. Before I could even let the judges speak or deny me, I began my audition. I guess success occurs when opportunity meets preparation.

I graduated with a BFA in acting from USC in 2019. During my time there I worked three jobs in order to support myself. There were days I would have to pick between buying a textbook or having groceries all week.

USC, although a place that rewarded me in so many ways, was also full of adversity. I would love to say that I am a working Latina actress, starring in two Netflix shows with a feature film coming out soon...but that's not the case. I hope that by the time you read this, it is.

BIOGRAPHY

Mayra A. Lozano is an actor who was born in Arandas Jalisco, Mexico, and was raised in southern California. She started theater at the age of 14 in high school and obtained two degrees in acting, one from the American Academy of Dramatic Arts and another, a bachelor of fine arts degree, from University of Southern California. She is currently represented by Kohner Agency, and managed by Industry Entertainment. In addition, Mayra runs a small art business, enjoys spending time with her family, is an advocate for Latinx voices in film, and loves horses.

FROM WALL STREET BUSINESSMAN TO HANDS-ON CHANGEMAKER

MARK LEROY MADRID

"Go the extra mile because there is no traffic there."

I grew up the son of migrant farm workers who picked cotton in a Texas farming community. Despite not being raised in an academic setting, with faith in God I muscled my way to high-achiever status in school because I intrinsically knew that education was my pathway to my purpose.

I knew if I worked hard and excelled, I would not only make my parents proud, but also open doors to distinguished opportunities. This drive catalyzed me to become the first Hispanic valedictorian in my town's history and to earn a full scholarship to the University of Texas at Austin where I majored in accounting and graduated with honors.

My limitless mindset did not stop there. Upon graduation from college, I landed my dream job as an investment banker on Wall Street. Subsequently, I was on my way to realizing another childhood dream of becoming bank president, and then the Great Recession hit.

Having to shut down a bank during this distressing period, I pivoted to my true purpose, catalyzing economic opportunity for all, especially in our Hispanic community nationwide.

I began my nonprofit career at the Houston Hispanic Chamber of Commerce (HHCC). Certainly, the nonprofit setting was the antithesis to my norm, but it was profound work that lifted our Latino community. Over time, I was promoted five times and became the first Chief Operations Officer (COO) in HHCC history.

Simultaneously, I began my pursuit of a master's in nonprofit administration at the University of Notre Dame Mendoza College of Business. As I completed my master's, I was appointed CEO of the Greater Austin Hispanic Chamber of Commerce.

Today I serve as CEO of the Latino Business Action Network (LBAN), a national nonprofit that collaborates with Stanford University to champion the Stanford Latino Entrepreneurship Initiative. LBAN's goal is to double the number of $10+ million, $100+ million, and $1+ billion Latinx businesses in the U.S. by 2025. This work is an American economic imperative and continues to fuel my purpose, passion, and energy daily. It is the highest honor imaginable to serve Latino and Latina entrepreneurs across the U.S. and Puerto Rico.

From my story, I hope others learn that our destiny is shaped not only from our achievements, but also our setbacks. It is important to discern that life is not linear and full of curveballs. The more we live, the more we learn to apply wisdom and the serenity prayer. While we do this, we must relentlessly pursue our purpose, our reason for being on this earth.

After many tragedies—including losing my father to COVID-19—I have found my purpose: to catalyze economic opportunity for all. This is what makes me a Hispanic Star. I have worked hard for everything I have achieved, but it has not been easy. I persevered with grit and *ganas*. Because I am a Hispanic Star, I will continue to go the extra mile because there is no traffic there. Ultimately, this mindset, God, and family are what make this Hispanic Star shine.

BIOGRAPHY

Mark Madrid is CEO of Latino Business Action Network, an organization with the goal of doubling the number of $10+ million Latinx businesses in the U.S. by 2025.

Previously, he served as CEO of the Greater Austin Hispanic Chamber of Commerce. He is a United States Army Honorary Colonel, Forbes Nonprofit Council member, and board member of the McCoy College of Business at Texas State University.

Mark is a recipient of many awards, such as the Jefferson Award, the University of Notre Dame Rev. Theodore M. Hesburgh Founder's Award, the University of Texas at Austin Community Legacy Award and the United States Hispanic Chamber of Commerce LGBT Advocate of the Year.

AIM HIGH, WORK HARD, AND DON'T LET YOUR CONTEXT DEFINE WHO YOU ARE

JESUS MANTAS

"The greatest danger for most of us is not that our aim is too high and we miss it, but that it is too low, and we reach it."

I landed in the United States of America on October 10, 1994, with a contract to work as a management consultant. I had been successful in Spain, earned national awards, graduated with honors, and served as an Officer in the Air Force of Spain.

A few weeks later, I was told I would not succeed in the U.S., especially as a management consultant. I was a "kid" who looked and sounded different, I could barely speak English, and some said I should change my name since the name "Jesus" might make people uncomfortable. I was then faced with the horrible choice many Hispanics face: do I want to be authentic, or do I want to fit in?

I chose to stay, and my journey swayed me from fitting in to being authentic. With hard work, conviction, and a bit of luck, I became an associate professor at the University of California,

Irvine, in the Graduate School of Management, one of the youngest consulting partners at PricewaterhouseCoopers, and the leader of large IBM businesses in North and Latin America.

In 2016, the "kid" that would not succeed as a management consultant, became the global general manager of IBM Business Consulting, one of the largest consulting organizations in the world. Today, I am a senior managing partner in the largest technology services organization in the world. I am also one of the few Hispanics sitting on a public company board of directors in the U.S. I work with the World Economic Forum in their global AI council, and I co-chair IBM's Hispanic Diversity Council.

And, to achieve these career milestones I didn't have to change my name.

I have been blessed by many great mentors, the hard-working discipline instilled in my upbringing, and many opportunities. I enjoy paying it forward and helping our Hispanic community thrive, and I would like to share three important factors for anyone's success:

First, aim higher than you think you can achieve. Michelangelo said, "The greatest danger for most of us is not that our aim is too high, and we miss it, but that it is too low, and we reach it." I was offered many opportunities and jobs that I was apprehensive to take, but great mentors saw my potential and convinced me I would succeed, even when I didn't see it. Surround yourself with the people that care about you and recognize your true potential.

Second, work harder than everyone around you and never stop learning. This is completely under your control and doesn't depend on birthright, genetics, or natural abilities. To sustain your hard work and continuous learning, choose a career aligned with your passion, so you are always working on something you love.

Last, but most importantly, don't ever let your context define who you are. You have the power to define yourself whether you are poor or accommodated. If life throws challenges your way, stay true to your authentic self.

Success is the outcome of an ensemble thriving together; it is rarely a solo act. We must dedicate equal time to helping others as we do to improving ourselves. My success is clearly only in small part due to me, and in great part due to the people who care about me.

BIOGRAPHY

Jesus Mantas is a Senior Managing Partner in IBM Services where he is responsible for global strategy, innovation, and corporate development for IBM's Global Business Services.

He has led IBM Business Consulting and IBM Business Process units, IBM GBS in Latin America and he is widely recognized for his ability to innovate and transform enterprises, and his expertise on design-led, technology powered, human-centric transformation.

Jesus serves on IBM's AI Ethics Board, IBM Services Board, and co-chairs IBM's Hispanic Diversity Council. He sits in the board of directors of Biogen Inc., the world leader in neuroscience. He was named one of the Top 25 Global Consulting Leaders by *Consulting Magazine* and has been recognized with other awards for his commitment to Hispanic diversity.

NADA

JESSE MARTINEZ

"NADA is impossible!"

It was March 1997 and this emerging network of the World Wide Web was my territory. I had just started my new job as employee number 27 in sales for a startup, Internet Systems Inc., based in Sunnyvale, California, which was funded by Sequoia Capital. Our company was one of two pioneers in the web hosting services space for marque internet brands such as Yahoo!, Netscape and others.

I earned top sales leader by closing key accounts such as USA Today, SGI, Electronic Arts, Softbank, and Ask Jeeves. I even won a briefcase with a thousand dollars all in ones at our company kick-off in Scottsdale, Arizona. In less than a year, we went from a startup to part of a public company, Frontier Communications, trading at $35 per share.

My strike price was 50 cents and this Tejano (from Houston) had now learned about tech stock options. I had discovered a whole new world in Silicon Valley, and it was the land of big visions and opportunities.

I resigned in fall 1998 to pursue my dream of launching my own startup with my brother, Edwardo. It was the beginning of Picosito.com – a bilingual portal serving the U.S. Hispanic Community, delivering culturally relevant content. Our motto was For Latinos, by Latinos. We raised around $2.3M in seed capital and launched on Cinco de Mayo, 1999. We were Latino pioneers in the Internet space delivering many firsts through our platform and receiving many accolades.

However, we lived the highs and lows of a startup and also as Latino founders. In six months after launching, we received an offer to be acquired for four million but kindly declined it. We had more work to do and value to deliver. Then we were presented another acquisition offer of more than eight million, then BUST! The stock market crashed in March 2000 and the acquisition offer evaporated.

The "Dot-com bust" was real--no more offers, no more growth capital. Our team was devastated. We continued to power through, but, ultimately, we had to face the reality of shutting down operations in December 2000.

Today I've been the founder of four startups and one nonprofit, Latino Startup Alliance, focused on empowering Latinx tech founders. It was that first startup that I joined in 1997, along with my entrepreneurial journey, that allowed me the opportunity to not only serve my fellow Latino entrepreneurs but to also be invited to The White House four times under tech inclusion, to speak at the Clinton Global Initiative, to attend two U.N. Summits, and then honored to attend Davos 2020 as part of the first U.S. Hispanic Delegation led by We Are All Human.

A son of immigrant parents (Alfred & Socorro) from Mexico, earning a bachelor of science in engineering from Texas A & M, and through the love and support from family, friends, mentors, champions, and advisors, it makes me extremely proud to be a Hispanic Star in helping to be of service to others.

Remember - *NADA is impossible!*

BIOGRAPHY

Jesse Martinez is a serial tech entrepreneur, educator, philanthropist, investor, advisor, mentor and a passionate evangelist for the global Latinx tech community. He was recently honored to attend the World Economic Forum 2020 in Davos as a delegate for the first U.S. Hispanic Delegation led by the We Are All Human Foundation.

FINDING MY PURPOSE

MARTY MARTINEZ

"Maybe you've been assigned this mountain to show others it can be moved."

It was the middle of December and I was on my flight to New York City to wrap up my last trip of 2019. Exhausted from a year of constantly traveling for work, I was looking forward to staying in Dallas for a while. I was on a solo flight to NYC for the second annual, Hispanic Leadership Summit at the United Nations, where Latino leaders from across the country would convene to advance the Hispanic agenda for the upcoming year.

Like many Latinos, I grew up with very humble beginnings. As a young girl, my mom grew up picking fruit and vegetables in 110-degree weather in the fields of Southern California. Born the second oldest in a family of six, I was the first in my family to graduate from high school and college.

Growing up in the barrio, I didn't know what a successful Latino looked like. I had never seen one in my life. I knew more people that went to prison than graduated high school. I had every reason to not be successful. But not to be deterred, I set out to break a generational curse that existed in being born into a family of immigrants.

When I started the Social Revolt Agency back in 2014, I was relentless in my pursuit of success, willing to do whatever it took for me to be the light for family and show them what is possible through hard work and a relentless pursuit for a better life.

Throughout 2019, I often found myself reflecting on some of life's most troubling questions. What is my purpose? Why am I here? As I sat on that plane, I realized for the first time that I had never taken a vacation since I started the company. It was the end of the year and now was the perfect time for me to book a solo trip to tackle life's toughest questions. So, I booked a solo trip to Switzerland to get my answers.

After a week of being alone in the Swiss Alps, I felt like I was just scratching the surface of those questions. Then I received a phone call from Claudia Romo Edelman, founder of We Are All Human. She saw I was in Switzerland and extended an opportunity that little did she know, gave me the answer I was seeking.

Claudia asked if I would be interested in being part of the first-ever, Hispanic delegation at the World Economic Forum in Davos, Switzerland, the following week to represent the U.S. Hispanic community on the global stage. A few hours later, I extended my trip for another week and headed for Davos.

As passionate as I am about what I do, marketing for me was never my purpose, but simply a vehicle for me to pull myself out of poverty and show others like me that if you think you can, you can. If you think you can't, you're right. As I write this, I am fulfilled in knowing my life's purpose is to be a shining light for the Hispanic community and help others see the greatness in themselves, even if they don't see it yet.

BIOGRAPHY

Marty Martinez is the CEO and Founder of Social Revolt Agency, a multicultural digital advertising agency with a focus on social media, web design, and paid strategy. Marty also works with the United Nations on global social impact initiatives and is passionate about being a voice for the Hispanic community.

SEE WHAT OTHERS DON'T SEE AND RAISE THEM UP TO HIGHER LEVELS!

YANETH MEDINA

"We have the power to lift others and if we unite in masses to do this, we can make a difference and help build a community of amazing leaders for this country."

It is 7:20 a.m. and I am sitting on a large board waiting for the senior leadership team to begin. My heart is racing. I was invited to the monthly meeting where the CEO and other executive officers review high level decisions about our bank. Being in this room was a BIG deal!

My inner self was excited to have made it this far, yet, as I looked around the room, I felt intimidated and that I did not belong there. Little did I know in that room, I had several advocates who knew I DID belong there. They knew what I could bring to the table and knew this would bring me new opportunities.

Fast forward 15 years later, and I am part of the Executive Team for a $1 billion asset bank. The CEO and I work closely together, and I am highly respected within the organization. I've worked hard to get here, and I love what I do. My passion to lead and elevate others is the greatest feeling of all. It is my mission to help transcend others in our organization and let them realize their talent. As John Calvin Maxwell, an American author, speaker, and pastor once said, 'What do all leaders have in common? They see more than others do and they see before others see."

You see, my advocates were the people who got me to that boardroom. They saw my talent, which I often questioned. They saw my potential and they were my sponsors. They challenged me, provided me with opportunities, and exposed me to decision makers to increase my visibility in the organization. As I moved up within the bank, I had the privilege to work with several executives who shared their insight about leadership and the power of elevating others.

One leader, in particular, holds a special place in my heart because he saw my potential, regularly reminded me of my potential, and showed my potential to others, as well. As leaders, this is what we should all be doing. We must advocate for our future leaders.

We have the power to lift others. If we unite in masses to do this, we can make a difference and help build a community of amazing leaders for this country. My parents used to say, "Tienes que ir a la escuela mija y trabajar duro para que puedes ser alguien en esta vida." Today, I can proudly say YES--sí soy alguien en esta vida y estoy ayudando a más gente para que ellos sean alguien también!

BIOGRAPHY

Yaneth Medina serves as Senior Vice President of Retail Banking and Head of Retail for St Charles Bank & Trust, a Wintrust Community Bank. She has more than 20 years of experience in retail banking, relationship building, workplace culture, and coaching and mentoring.

She also dedicates her time to serving several organizations in the local area including the Centro De Informacion, Elgin Area Chamber of Commerce, and Marklund.

Yaneth's family consists of her three wonderful boys, her parents, and her brother and sister. They have been her inspiration!

THE SELF-WORTH MY MOTHER TAUGHT ME

CHRISTIAN "KIKI" MELENDEZ

"God inspires you to be who you are meant to be; the meaning of life is to have the faith and courage to pursue it!"

I was raised by a single mother, but everyone would always tell me, "Your mother didn't take crap from any man." I never knew what that meant, but as I got older, I started to realize.

The biggest turning point in my life reads like a romance novel. I think it was 1995. I was a radio DJ in New York City, and was asked to cover a press conference for the new soccer team that was being announced.

I arrived and the room was full of reporters; the team stood center stage. During the press conference, one player made eye contact with me across the room. He was drop dead gorgeous. I couldn't imagine why he was looking at me, so I looked around to make sure. He mouthed in front of everyone, "What's your name?"

I was mortified. Everyone's eyes went directly to me, and

the coach speaking was evidently annoyed. Needless to say, I fell in love instantly, and we were inseparable from that day on. I had always dreamed of moving to LA to pursue my career in film and television, but now I just wanted to be with ALEX for the rest of my life.

About two and a half months into the relationship, we were walking into a restaurant and he opened the big, heavy, glass-framed oak wood door, walked in, and forgot I was right behind him. The door swung towards me and I froze. Miraculously, the door stopped a centimeter short of my nose. I was shaken, but he looked back without any regard for what had just happened.

When we sat down, I asked him, "Didn't you see how the door almost killed me?"

"So, what, nothing happened right?" he replied, and opened the menu.

"Don't you understand that your rudeness almost hurt me?" I insisted.

"Just shut up and order," he replied.

Everything changed in that moment, but I acted like all was well. The minute I walked into my apartment, I broke down crying and asked God for a sign. The song *Fantasy* by Earth, Wind and Fire started playing full blast, the song lyrics counseling me. *Take a plane far away to a land called Fantasy.*

I realized I had to go back to plan A. I do believe God inspires you to be who you are meant to be; the meaning of life is to have the faith and courage to pursue it!

So I took a pen and wrote a note: "Please help me make my

dreams come true...selling everything to move to L.A." I posted it in my elevator for all my neighbors to see. The next day they came and bought me out. I packed my clothes and headed to L.A. I never saw Alex again, although I heard he was going crazy looking for me.

It was the most empowering thing I have ever done. Now, I am married with twins and living my dream in L.A.!

BIOGRAPHY

Christian "Kiki" Melendez has been writing and creating content for television and film for over 20 years. Her first docu-comedy, *Journey of a Female Comic*, received critical acclaim and was Oscar-qualified in 2015. After a theatrical release, this movie is on Amazon Prime and multiple platforms.

She has created, produced and aired multiple television projects for both markets on a national level, such as top-rated *Kiki Desde Hollywood* on Galavision, The All-Female Comedy Special, *Hot Tamales Live* on Showtime Networks, *Locos Y Contentos* on Estrella TV and *Kiki Mobile* on A&E's FYI Networks.

Currently, she is the founder of Omni Cultural TV Fest, a unique, one-of-a-kind television expo that celebrates diversity and inclusion. She will become an author this fall (2020) with the release of her first book *Chase Hope & Faith.*

STILL I RISE

MARISEL MELENDEZ

"We are survivors; we are going to make it!"

Growing up with a single mother of three who realized early that in order to make it in this world we had to work hard without taking shortcuts--that is what makes my mother the owner of the most successful Puerto Rican restaurant in Chicago, Ponce Restaurant. Ponce's 22-year history began out of the trunk of my mother's car.

Just like my mother, I, too, became a single mother, but with different challenges. Even with all of the obstacles, I still managed to finish high school, three children later. I then got my medical assistant degree, landed a full-time job in the medical industry, and after a decade, when my fourth child was just turning two, I pivoted and joined my mom to help her run the restaurant.

As my children grew up and started families of their own, it was very important to me that they knew I would always be there for them. I faced many of the common problems that parents face when having kids. Child after child, problem after problem, I would often remind myself that our children need their parents, no matter what. They were my "WHY" and I would never leave their side.

I remember when my son had arteriovenous malformation (AVM), a bunch of tangled blood vessels in the brain that ruptured at the age of 23. "You're a great dad." These were my last words to him as they rolled him into surgery.

I knew those words would give him the strength to fight and survive to be around for his daughter. And he was, a few years later, when his six-year-old daughter survived a bullet to the chest, where the bullet remains forever lodged just inches away from her heart.

My son is a survivor, my granddaughter is a survivor, and so is my grandson, who just months after being born has undergone heart surgery to repair two heart murmurs. As a family, we have overcome countless struggles. This is why Destiny's Child song lyrics resonate with me. *"I'm a survivor, I'm not going to give up, I'm not going to stop, I'm going to work harder, I'm a survivor!"*

Every day I continue to strive to be a great mother and daughter. My mother was on a mission with all her kids by her side and never gave up, in spite of the obstacles she had to endure. I too have often thought, we are survivors; we are going to make it.

Today, I am the face of *Ponce Restaurant* and it has everything to do with the scars that I've picked up along the way that enables me to connect with all walks of life. I have created a whole social media campaign called "Ponce Life." I even co-host *BoricuaTalks,* a YouTube sensation.

All because I believed in me, even when all the odds were

against me, with teen pregnancy and a broken nose. My scars will forever remind me that I was destined for greatness, and so are you. Don't ever let your circumstances define who you are or who you want to become.

BIOGRAPHY

Marisel Melendez is a mother to four beautiful children and eight grandchildren. You can always find her at *Ponce Restaurant,* doing Facebook Live videos of the delicious food, live music, and family ambiance.

When she's not at Ponce or spending quality time with her family, she is recording for *BoricuaTalks, a show about nothing and a little bit about everything.*

Marisel has always had a passion for reading and journaling. She is a co-author in *Today's Inspired Latina, Volume IV*, which has introduced her to some amazing women. Currently, she is writing her personal memoir.

NEVER LET ANYONE ELSE DEFINE WHO YOU ARE

CARMEN MILAGRO

"I'm everything that I choose to be, and I choose to be me!"

From the day I entered my kindergarten classroom, I knew I was different, but it was more of a feeling rather than a realization that my looks set me apart from the other children. I couldn't actually "see" myself as others saw me. It never occurred to me that "they" might judge me because of the color of my skin or because my hair was a thick, dark, almost blue-black perfect cascade that caught the sunlight when I walked by. I simply noted that no one else spoke Spanish.

In my mind's eye, I was like every other child, as I walked, skipped, ran, stumbled, jumped, played, and studied. One thing that did indeed set me apart from everyone else was that at home, I spoke only Spanish, ate Salvadorian foods and was raised fully immersed in my culture and in the traditions of my parent's country. School was teaching me so much more about a different world.

This world was called the United States of America, the home of the free and the place where I was born.

By second grade, with the help of my extraordinary teachers, I had caught up and could speak, read, understand, and write English perfectly for my age group. I became a voracious reader and have remained one to this day. I devoured all types of books and by the time I was in third grade, I had traveled to dozens of countries and discovered many magical kingdoms, through my imagination and by way of the stories I loved to read. I knew then, that one day I would travel the world, and I have been very fortunate to have indeed, traveled and sailed to many, many different places around the globe.

When I reached fourth grade, my life changed forever because Miss Carr, my teacher was an "artist." Every lesson she taught was based on some form of art. As an adult, I have never been able to figure out how she used art for every subject, but she did. It was in the middle of her classroom, one bright sunny afternoon, while we were busy painting, that I, too, became an artist.

Since that day, starting at the age of nine, I have never identified or thought of myself as anything other than an artist. Artists have no skin color, no gender, and no need for any other label. An artist is simply an artist and I chose that identity for myself. No one else did. It was my decision. My choice.

THIS is what made me different and special. This was the beginning of how I have moved through the world and lived my life never caring what other people thought of me and why I have NEVER subscribed to their labels. I'm everything that I choose to be, and I choose to be me!

At the age of 40, I chose to be known as an entrepreneur-artist named Carmen Milagro.

BIOGRAPHY

Carmen Milagro is a first-generation San Franciscan, an entrepreneur-artist, pragmatic visionary, certified CBD-educator, confidence strategist, and coach, plus businesswoman, mentor, inventor, patent-holder, storyteller, director, producer, advocate for women's successes, and creator of a premium hemp CBD lifestyle brand. She is also a HISPA (Hispanics Inspiring Students' Performance and Achievement) role model, consultant to SF Music City to inspire the next generation of young musicians, and hosts Confidence Strategies 101, CBD With YOUR Favorite PhD, and co-hosts Yo Soy Latina.

Carmen is an expert content writer for *Live & Thrive and Better Health & Wellness* magazines and is a spokesperson, international entertainer, lyricist and philanthropist.

HISPANIC DIVERSITY

JEANETTE V. MIRANDA

"I am arroz con gandules y un Cafecito Cubano."

Lucy: I don't think it's very nice of you making fun of my Spanish.

Ricky: Well, you've been making fun of my English for fifteen years.

Lucy: That's different, Spanish is a foreign language.

Ricky: English is a foreign language to me.

Lucy: Well, the way you speak it, it is to me too."

In the 1950s, the U.S. Hispanic population was one percent of the total population. The I Love Lucy show introduced the first Hispanic, a Cuban actor playing a Cuban with a thick accent, who was half of an intercultural couple, along with an American woman named Lucy.

On the show, Ricky Ricardo spoke about being marginalized, and most of all, being misunderstood when he spoke. U.S. history shows that Hispanics had lived in what is now the U.S. since before any colonization from England on the East coast ever happened. From Florida to the Pacific Ocean to the Canadian border, Hispanic and Spanish cultures have been around since 1565. Spain established the harbor town of St. Augustine, Florida, the first European settlement in what was eventually to become the United States.

Just like Lucy and Desi's experience, in my marriage, there is a cultural divide. I was born in the USA to Puerto Rican parents. My husband, Orlando, was born in Cuba and arrived in Chicago when he was eight years old. He learned English hard and fast, via television, friends, and school. I learned English from my cousins, TV, and the bilingual program at school. We both learned Spanish from our parents and extended family.

The cultural divide in our home has been about the expression of words, food, and music. Hispanics are categorized as a homogeneous group because they all speak the Spanish language. But nothing could be further from the truth.

Hispanics are not a monolithic group either; they differ by acculturation and assimilation as well as a country of origin. Hispanics come from 20 different countries of origin that speak Spanish, and they all eat a different version of rice! In part, each group has its own different behaviors, idiosyncrasies, views, and idiomatic expressions.

For example, the word bus is said differently among Hispanics. Caribbeans say *"la guagua"*, Uruguayans say, *"el omnibus"*, and Mexicans say, *"el camion"*. There are many words that Cubans and Puerto Ricans express differently, too. The first time I asked my husband to hand over the *"frisa"*, he did not understand what I was asking. Frisa, to me, is a blanket. In his culture, they say *"colcha"*. For many years, we would argue about what food we would make for Nochebuena, Cuban or Puerto Rican cuisine.

We all add to each other's *sazon*. In our household, we have acculturated. I am *arroz con gandules y un Cafecito Cubano!* Now my husband says, *"Frisa!"* As for *Nochebuena*, we alternate the feast every year. I'm a little bit *guaguancó*, Orlando is a little bit *bomba y plena*, and we both are a little bit rock-n-roll.

BIOGRAPHY

Jeanette V. Miranda has simultaneously owned and managed businesses ranging from a children's boutique shop, a Cuban restaurant, a digital advertising display screen company to a marketing agency.

For 23 years, she was co-owner of Miranda Hispanic Marketing, a fully integrated marketing, public relations, and promotional agency. She was the director of multicultural marketing, working with an array of clients such as Anheuser-Busch, Miller Brewing Company, Sprint, and Novamex-Jarritos.

Jeanette currently presides as president of the board of directors for Latino Treatment Center. She published her applied research thesis for her master's degree, *E-commerce Marketing Services to the Growing U.S. Hispanics Market: Issues and Implications that Come with Major Population Change.*

THE OBSTACLE IS THE WAY

ELAINE MONTILLA

"I knew early on that education was my passport, and I decided that I would add as many stamps as I could."

The decision to come to the United States from the Dominican Republic was not a complicated one for my mom. Coming to the U.S. was our only option, and in a matter of weeks I had to attend a new school and learn a language that I only heard in movies growing up.

Ever since, obstacles have always shown me that the reward on the other side was always greater than the fear that wanted to paralyze me. It was hard learning a new language, it was embarrassing being singled out because of my accent or my curly hair, and it was even worse when I knew all the answers to the math questions, but didn't have a way of explaining it.

I knew early on that education was my passport, and I decided that I would add as many stamps as I could, to ensure I could develop my talents and have skills to help my growth. I always heard that knowledge was power, but I fully understood it when I got my first job in tech.

I knew that knowledge would make people look beyond my accent, the color of my skin, or my curly hair. I know that my degrees helped me succeed and get promoted over and over again. I went from being a help desk technician that was on-call 24 hours, to a help desk supervisor, a help desk manager, then to IT director, and from there to assistant vice president.

Each step of the way, I had to work 20 times harder than the person next to me. I had to stay up late and always provide more than what was asked of me. Some people run away when things get difficult, but I stare at it, and even talk to it while asking, "What lesson are you here to teach me?" I consider myself a life-long student, and even today I focus on hiring people who are smarter than me. When my dreams seemed far because I was afraid to speak in public, I joined a group to practice and to challenge the old view I had of myself.

Nobody is born knowing it all, and I knew at a young age that I could learn anything I set my mind to if I worked hard and practiced enough. Today, I am the chief information officer at a prestigious university, and I thank the many challenges that helped me get here. I know I can overcome hard challenges and also know that you can too.

Meditation, journaling, and self-love, plus having amazing mentors in my life helped me be where I am today. My accent, the color of my skin, my curls, and being Latina are all my superpowers, and you can make them yours, too. Just remember, the obstacle is the way and each one helped me become a Hispanic Star.

BIOGRAPHY

Elaine Montilla is the Assistant Vice President and CIO for IT at The Graduate Center, CUNY, a Forbes Technology Council member/contributor, and an AMA Women's Leadership Center presenter.

She is an accomplished senior executive with two decades as an IT leader in higher education. Montilla is also a TEDx speaker and the founder of 5xminority.com, a blog and social media brand dedicated to empowering women and minorities, especially in tech.

Elaine is skilled in educational technology, IT strategy, management, system deployment, and project portfolio management and recognized for staff professional development, change leadership, and talent for communicating with diverse groups of people.

TAMIKA LECHEÉ MORALES

"Inclusion is making a new space, a better space for everyone."

"I'd take a bullet for you." You'd only dare to vocalize such a cliché if you loved someone so much that you would literally sacrifice life and limb to save what you love and hold so dear. Anything less just wouldn't suffice.

When my Legend was born, he entered this world blue with the umbilical cord wrapped around his neck, hanging on to life and fighting to stay alive. This wouldn't be the first fight we faced together. Nearly five years later, a doctor uttered three words that would change the trajectory of our lives forever: Autism Spectrum Disorder.

See, I'm used to fighting. I've fought my whole life to be where I am today. I was the first in my household to graduate high school, then graduate college with honors and a four-year-old son, and still go on to earn my master's degree with a perfect 4.0 GPA.

By 33, I owned a few homes, cars, and my own franchise

business while working as a full-time schoolteacher. If that wasn't enough, I pivoted my spare-time dream of acting into more of a full-time passion, and then I added playwriting into the mix.

I had this undeniable GRIT and a tenacity for taking risks which I credit completely to being raised in a two-bedroom apartment in the projects of New York with 10 other relatives who were not my mom or dad. I learned how to trust my instincts and survive everything that came my way. But "autism" was different. It literally knocked the wind out of my stride. I felt paralyzed. For two years, I was completely lost.

Then, I'd like to say that I had an awakening. Writing helped me heal and reflect and that was the genesis of The Autism Hero Project, a 501c3 not-for-profit that serves to "prepare kids with autism for the world and the world for them."

I realized that autism awareness wasn't enough if it did not make you intentional about being an agent of change. With a prevalence of 1 in 54 children in the U.S. being diagnosed with autism, it is our collective duty to intentionally make space and be inclusive of those with neurodivergent brains and to help the world understand that neurodiversity should not be looked at as "less," "flawed," or "damaged goods." This negative stigma is what prevents us from seeing these beautiful humans as our equals and all that they have to teach us.

Inclusion takes work and commitment. It is not a one-time prescription where you hold a training, maybe even hire that one employee, and think that you can now check it off your list. It must be embedded in the culture, in every business system and process.

Inclusion is not bringing people into what already exists. Inclusion is making a new space, a better space for everyone. This only comes with being intentional about hiring and retaining people with special needs. You will have to be a little creative and put some work into it, but as Hispanics, this is already ingrained in us.

I am determined to make a world that is inclusive of my son and those like him and for that, I need you.

BIOGRAPHY

Comcast Newsmakers, Fox News, Univision, Telemundo and WGN9 – Chicago's Very Own are just a few of the media outlets that have featured this *"Firessa"*, Tamika Lecheé Morales.

She was also selected as *Today's Inspired Latina* Woman of the Year in 2018 and has served as a keynote speaker and emcee for various events. Tamika serves her community primarily as a dual language teacher and president of The Autism Hero Project (AHP).

As an actress, Tamika has been fortunate to play several leading roles by inspiring Latinx playwrights. Tamika is passionate about serving humanity by raising cultural awareness, invoking thought, and raising consciousness in the hearts and minds of audiences. Her acting career became the catalyst for sharing her life stories as a playwright and co-author for the book series, *Today's Inspired Latina Volume III: Life Stories of Success in the Face of Adversity* published in May 2017.

REJECTION, "ME DA GANAS", AND MY KEY TO SUCCESS

LAURA MORENO LUCAS

"Juntos todos podemos subir apoyándonos unos a los otros."

In September of 2019, I stood next to my family as I rang the Nasdaq bell in their Times Square headquarters in honor of Hispanic Heritage Month, which was broadcast to the extended Latino network and Latin America on Univision. A seminal moment in my career and life, my event honored Latino leadership in the world's financial center.

Six months later, I left Nasdaq. Crushed, but not broken.

Why? Let me start at the beginning. I grew up in rural Cuidad Guzman, Mexico. At my grandparent's farm, we spoke only Spanish. At a young age, we moved to Vacaville, California.

My new school terrified me. I spoke no English, but an unlikely savior emerged in the person of an elderly janitor, Jesse, who was the only one in school who knew both Spanish and English.

My parents spoke little English, so I stayed after school and Jesse would patiently tutor me. Helping me navigate through elementary school, he was someone who took the time to help me absorb English, and his kindness changed my life. That seminal experience helped me develop internal resilience. It would be needed.

After the accolades for the Nasdaq bell event faded, others within the company told me they did not believe I could sustain my record. As more doors closed for me to succeed, I did what any *tapitia*, proud Latina woman, and entrepreneur would do. I started my own company.

I was no stranger to rejection. After graduating from college, I yearned to be an FBI agent, but they told me I was too inexperienced.

I loved to dance, auditioning in New York for Broadway plays. I made it to the final 50 of the Oakland Raiderettes Cheerleaders tryouts. They cut me saying that I couldn't "kick high enough," and besides, they had other Latinas in the squad.

I was a finalist on the CNBC series, "SharkTank," and they cut me because the subscription boutique company I pitched had less subscribers than another similar company they favored.

Rejection is a part of everyone's life. But it is how you power through the resulting doubts and fears that make the difference.

As a Latina, I fell prey to "the imposter syndrome," where I knew someone would see only my flaws, not my strengths. But as long as I persevered, nothing could stop me. I made the conscious choice to meet challenges with compassion and kindness, which would ultimately open other doors for me.

Today, I focus on offering fully bilingual content to increase awareness on the capital markets within diverse communities. We all need the opportunity to have access, not just Wall Street insiders.

Together we can all rise while supporting each other. My passion for building a resilient world, broadening access to economic parity for women, especially minorities, inspires me every day.

BIOGRAPHY

Laura Moreno Lucas is a Latina entrepreneur and founder of Pandocap, a media company demystifying the capital markets. Pandocap brings you quick clips and easy-to-understand information, giving every community equal access to top-line intelligence with bilingual content.

As former managing director for New Listings and Capital Markets at Nasdaq, Laura helped companies and entrepreneurs navigate from private to public markets. Her background also includes time as a top sales executive at Salesforce and more than ten years at financial firms, including TD Ameritrade and Sungard.

Between finance and tech roles, Laura founded Ladada, one of the first startup fashion subscription services, featuring emerging new designers.

A TALE OF TWO HOMES

MARCIA MORENO

"My two homes keep me grounded, aware, and grateful."

I want to tell you my story. It may not be like the ones you hear on the news, but it is my story, and we, as immigrants, need to start sharing more often.

I was born and raised in Chile. Five years after graduating college, a once-in-a-lifetime opportunity to pursue a graduate degree in the United States came, thanks to a visionary friend and mentor. Once I got to Cleveland, I was on a mission: study hard for two years, then head back home. Not even once did I think I would stay.

Being in my 20s, I thought I knew it all. Little did I know what would happen in the next few years. My husband at that time came with me to Cleveland, and soon after arriving, got depressed and homesick. We got divorced two years later.

I realized that no book, movie, or TV show prepares you for what you go through when you have to start a life in another country. I had to accept that English will never be my native language, and there would be things I cannot fully express. I had to accept that I will always be an outsider, that my life as I knew it had changed forever, and I would never feel totally "at home" anywhere again.

I have been in Cleveland for 15 years. I am married now, and I have a 7-year-old boy. Every day I learn how to live with my heart split in two. It took all my courage to leave everything behind and start from scratch. I don't regret it, but it is not easy and never will be. My heart is divided between two homes, two countries, two cultures, and two families that are never going to be able to connect. Me and my son will be that connector.

Last summer, I took my son on a two-month-long vacation to Chile. After such an intense trip, the first week back was strange. He said, "Mama, home seems different, like another world. It's like I don't live here."

With every trip it is becoming harder to understand who I am, who he is, and where we belong; it's a curse and a blessing. A curse because I want to be here when I am there and vice versa; my parents are not here to see my son grow or when I am sick. I have missed weddings, births, christenings, and funerals.

But it is mostly a blessing. I have learned to be flexible, innovative, resourceful, resilient; I navigate two cultures in two languages without forgetting who I am and becoming someone different at the same time. I am now more open to change, to the unknown, to the uncertainty.

I am thankful for what I have. My two homes keep me

grounded, aware, and grateful. I will never forget that Cleveland opened its arms and gave me a home; and I will never forget where I come from.

BIOGRAPHY

Marcia Moreno is a self-driven, passionate, bilingual professional with more than 15 years of experience in human resources, workforce development, diversity, inclusion and equity.

In 2018, she founded AmMore Consulting LLC, dedicated to creating more diverse, inclusive, and equitable workplaces by supporting organizations to become Latinx-ready.

Marcia came to the U.S. in 2005 to pursue a graduate degree at Cleveland State University, and since then she has dedicated her career to empowering Latinx to become a true economic and cultural force. She is deeply and passionately involved in various local organizations such as the Young Latino Network, College Now, and Global Cleveland, among others.

FIGHTING IMPOSTER SYNDROME

JESSICA MUÑOZ

"Like the monarch butterfly, I learned to go confidently and fearlessly into the path the Lord has created for me."

The sun's rays warmed my skin and my soul. As I looked up, I noticed a majestic monarch butterfly. It flew confidently and fearlessly into the infinite sky and she transferred peaceful energy to my inner core. This was my daily reminder that I was brave enough to face my fears...that I was not an imposter in medical school.

My first two years of medical school were mentally and emotionally challenging. I felt out of place because very few students looked like me, and this made me doubt my potential to become a physician. My free time was swept away and replaced by studying eight to ten hours a day. I was sleeping an average of six hours a night, and my anxiety was out of control and causing severe insomnia.

When I was preparing for my nine-hour medical licensing exam, I experienced the death of multiple family members. Despite the emotional toll this took on my mental health, I continued to study. Unfortunately, not achieving my target scores led me to believe that I was a failure. In spite of graduating *summa cum laude* from college and representing my class as commencement speaker, I still doubted my accomplishments and my intelligence. Was I smart enough to become a physician?

Despite the constant anxiety, insomnia, and the doubts and intense fears, I continued to study. I quickly realized that my deteriorating mental health was hindering my ability to be the learner I knew I could be. Therefore, I decided to take time off from medical school and take care of my soul. I prayed every day and gave my worries to God. I taught myself self-care, learned to trust God, engaged in cognitive behavioral therapy, started boxing, and writing a book. My existence was bigger than a medical licensing exam and I was committed to taking care of me.

Learning how to prioritize my mental health was rejuvenating. When I returned to medical school, I enjoyed learning and stayed committed to my happiness. My third and fourth year of medical school allowed me to enjoy the learning process without the anxiety. I finally felt like I belonged in the field of medicine. I was no longer doubting my abilities to succeed as a future Latina physician. I learned that I had the willpower, endurance, and intelligence to become a physician, and even though I didn't see physicians who looked like me, I would pave the way for other future minority physicians.

My fearless, compassionate personality resonates deeply with the demands that emergency medicine physicians face on a daily basis. My endurance will ensure that I remain focused and alert during residency, whereas my advocacy skills will enable my patients to trust me in order to make life-saving decisions.

Do not let your fears and doubts shatter your dreams. You owe it to yourself to keep fighting. *Tu puedes.* Like the monarch butterfly, I learned to go confidently and fearlessly into the path the Lord has created for me.

BIOGRAPHY

Jessica Muñoz is the daughter of immigrants from Michoacán, Mexico. She was born and raised in Illinois.

She is currently a fourth-year medical student at the Ohio State University College of Medicine, specializing in emergency medicine.

In her spare time, Jessica is a social justice and mental health advocate.

THE DAY PIQUITO DE ORO DIED IN CHICAGO

ANTONIO NUÑEZ

"You could say that I found my new self in my Spanish accent, or that my accent finally found me."

This time I landed in Chicago. I had just been hired by an advertising agency specifically because I was good with words. I have been a "pico de oro" (silver tongue) since I was a kid. Being a professional public speaker was my profession in Spain, where I was born.

My first day at work. The ad agency was at the Merchandise Mart, the world's biggest building in 1930. It's a structure so gigantic that it has its own zip code. After half an hour wandering around those art-deco corridors and stumbling upon the same bronze bust for the third time, I had to do what men hate most: admit that I was utterly lost. I stopped a good Samaritan, and did the second thing men hate most, asked for directions.

The instant I pronounced a few words, the chap looked at my mouth in shock. The more I spoke, the more he looked at it, staring with a mix of confusion and genuine curiosity. I felt that he was about to grab my chin and open my mouth wide to study it. Instead, he decided to leave. Then, I tried asking a middle-aged woman. All I could understand, from what I perceived to be gibberish, was that she was very, very sorry. Finally, I spotted someone who was brown like me. This Latino executive patiently answered my question, vocalizing to perfection.

"YOUR-ACCENT-IS-SO-THICK-THAT-I-CAN-NOT-UNDERSTAND-A-WORD," he said. *"Pues hablemos español"*, I replied. "SORRY-I-DON'T-SPEAK-SPANISH," he said.

I was perplexed. My first stint in the U.S. had been in Miami, and nobody ever had an issue with my accent there. Besides, if the executive was Latino, was it true that he didn't speak Spanish? In the Midwest, what in Miami sounded fluid, like Mozart, it landed as an Egyptian hieroglyphic. I learned the hard way the assumptions people can make when you have a Latino accent.

"Piquito de oro" died. I lost my confidence and self-esteem. I was not me anymore. The worst part was, I had no clue who I could be in my new country.

It took me years to accept that, no matter how many books, teachers, or accent programs I studied, I would always have an accent. I had to renegotiate my identity. I learned that there is beauty in my accent, and that difference can be a strength. I learned that having an accent is profoundly American because this country was built by people with accents from all over the world.

Today I work in a New York consultancy that helps companies understand our rich Latino culture. I help people and brands who want to listen, for their first time, to people with an accent. I connect them with Latinos who speak English with an accent, Latinos who don't speak English, Latinos who speak Spanish with an accent, and Latinos who don't speak a word of Spanish. You could say that I found my new self in my Spanish accent, or that my accent finally found me.

BIOGRAPHY

Antonio Nuñez is an author, speaker, and culture-driven communication consultant for clients like AB InBev, Johnson & Johnson, and Unilever.

He was awarded the Advertising Efficacy Grand Prix and the Napolitan Victory Award for the best political book. He was born in Spain but is an honorary citizen of the world. More info at antonionunez.com

FAITH IN THE UNCERTAINTY

GINA PARDIÑO

"Faith is a substance of things we hope for, it is knowing that things are real even if we do not see them (Hebrews 11:1 ERV)."

It was an early Saturday morning when a little voice in my head pushed me to attend the youth service of my church. I was supposed to stay at home to study for my test to pass nursing school. I had been struggling for the entire semester in my medical surgical course. I knew I had to get at least an 83 percent or above to move on to the last semester and graduate.

I remember being so angry with God. Working hard every day and thinking how wrong of him it was to take it all away. During the prayer session, I was literally yelling at God in my thoughts for all the uncertainty that I had been feeling. I remember thinking that I was not sure what in the world he was doing. But I needed an answer and I needed it at that moment. God answered me instantly as the pastor shared the title of his message, which showed the word "finish" on the projector.

There are times when it seems like God or the universe stops you from reaching something you so desperately want to accomplish. For me, graduating nursing school meant more than just becoming a nurse. It meant that I would be the first in my family to graduate from college, to be part of the 3.6 percent of Hispanic nurses in the nation, the one to inspire my sister to go back to school, and to make my parents proud. I had surpassed so many obstacles along the way that I was near the end of it all by graduation.

I look back on that Saturday morning as a day to reflect on. I was positive that God reminded me to finish what I started, no matter how difficult it got. I had to stay hopeful that things would work out in the end. So, it did, and more than what I expected. I took my exam and passed with an 87 percent. In addition, my professor was able to return points from previous exams which helped to increase my grade. Since then, I have graduated, and I am blessed to be working in such an honorable profession.

Faith is a substance of things we hope for, it is knowing that things are real even if we do not see them (Hebrews 11:1 ERV). I may not see my future clear as day, but despite all uncertainty, remaining faithful to what I desire helps me to reach my goals. Of course, some plans do not happen. However, I see them as a possibility that there is something else in store for me, rather than a disadvantage.

Life is full of surprises, so just imagine what a little faith can do if it is known to move mountains!

BIOGRAPHY

Gina Aridai Pardiño is proud to share two cultures as a Mexican American. She is blessed to be living a life of serving those in need as a registered nurse, sharing her story as a contributing author, and inspiring those around her as a motivational speaker!

DREAMS WITHOUT COLOR, RACE OR RELIGION

ADRIANA PEÑA

"The color of your skin is not your obstacle; always be curious, inquire, and broaden your perspective on life."

It was a weekend after July 4, 1999, when I set foot on North American land; I was 19 years old and had many longings to fulfill. My story may or may not be as common as that of those who immigrate to the United States. Although being honest, I never intended to be doing what I love to do. From the time I arrived, I dedicated myself to work and study, and to return to my country of origin, but after three years, I knew very well that I would not return...at least not on my own.

Like all young women at that age, I was full of desire for personal growth; but soon I realized that there was always someone who wanted to keep me quiet about my ideas, making me feel insecure. What they did not know was that my curiosity and my desires would be stronger than their words; so, with fear and shyness but with a lot of determination, I went ahead with my dreams, learning about my interests.

I studied programming because I have always loved technology. I took online courses on graphic design and web pages. As technology and social media expanded, I grew creatively. But none of that made me feel fulfilled, until I started painting in 2010. Experimenting with artistic techniques, I felt that I had found what I really loved.

In 2013, I exhibited for the first time at an auction event and my piece sold. I was very excited. From there, I decided to become part of the artist community. I have been part of exhibitions in New York, on the streets of downtown Chicago, Pilsen, Back of the Yards, Cicero, Berwyn and other suburbs. As a muralist, I am proud that one of my murals is displayed in the Pokémon Go app. I have had the opportunity to work with adults with different abilities in a nonprofit organization well loved by the community. My determination to share my roots turned me into a Mexican embroidery instructor at Pilsen Arts Community House.

I am a member of the collective *"Mujeres Mutantes"* where we share our artistic experiences with young people and other artists; we currently reside at Hyde Park Art Center. Thanks to *Mujeres Latinas en Acción* I learned how to run a business and develop a brand; my daughter and I create designs for everyday items. I know that *"Meshikanita"* will prosper one day. Wow, after listening to me, I feel happy because I don't feel more or less than anyone. I feel like a woman full of achievements thanks to being curious.

So, remember that when you listen in a derogatory tone, "Your skin is very dark," or "You are very short," or "You will not be able," or "That is impossible," or "I cannot help you"...then, you must close your eyes, listen to your inner being, and just let yourself grow professionally. The color of your skin is not your obstacle; always be curious, inquire, and broaden your perspective on life. Don't let anyone tell you that you can't.

BIOGRAPHY

Adriana Peña is a Chicago-based artist who was born in Mexico. She immigrated to the United States in 1999. Upon her arrival, she experimented with many new American trends but never lost her strong Mexican roots.

Seeking to calm her deep longing for her homeland, she experimented with most of the visual art techniques on a personal level. In 2013, she began to show her work in public and at many local and national art exhibitions.

Although her work is inspired largely by her love of Mexico, it is also an expression of her personal belief and admiration as well as respect and love for nature. These elements are an essential part of her current works of art.

HOW A MAGICAL ENDING STARTED BY A MOUSE

LILIAN PEÑA

"Each of us has a unique part to play in the healing of the world." -Marianne Williamson

As a kid, I lay on our living room floor with my light-blue Mickey Mouse record player. His hand held the needle which I would carefully place on the small record to start the story. I'd observed my dad position the needle ever so carefully on the Camilo Sesto LP, blasting his album, and now I recall the song, *"Jamás."*

My hand held a *Little Golden Book* to follow along, reading the story in English. I was born in San Francisco, the product of an immigration journey – my mom flew in on a plane, my dad followed on foot through borders, unlawfully, eventually leading to citizenship.

My early years drew me to the Disney brand. It was what my parents considered part of the American Dream. In addition to my record player, I got a Mickey Mouse radio (yellow with Mickey laying atop) and a Mickey jean bag. In 1977, I experienced the gift of a lifetime, a trip to Disneyland, which I relive through old photographs (my dad owned a camera like a true journalist, to capture stories).

Through those picture windows, I see family adventures in *It's a Small World*, my grandfather with Goofy, and my mother with old-fashioned Mickey Mouse. I didn't know at the time, which makes it even more magical, that in my professional life in 2015, I would tour the park behind-the-scenes for the 60th Diamond anniversary. It was then that I experienced my first (of two) Robert "Bob" Iger sightings.

I was accepted into the 2013-2014 Disney mentoring program as a rising star. If you know the scene from Adam Sandler's *Spanglish*, he issued a challenge to three kids to find sand glass and the young Latina found the most by staying out until dusk, collecting pieces from the beach. Well, I was that young Latina, during the classes in the presence of high-level executives, eagerly taking notes.

At the end of the nine-month program, I ended up with a thick document of Disney insights. Learning aside, walking through The Lot was amazing. I remember one particular day, I chose to wear a flowing, burgundy dress with shining accessories. I caught the attention of the Latino gardeners – I didn't know how to feel, yet I sashayed my way to The Rotunda restaurant for lunch with my corporate communications mentor. A few tables away was Anne Sweeney, a division leader at the time, who would give the program closing speech.

Later in my Disney life, in 2019, I travelled back to the same Lot area for diversity and inclusion meetings. As I walked out of the Frank G. Wells plaza toward the Team Disney Building, I saw him for the second time. My inner voice spoke out loud, "Oh, look, it's Bob Iger," to which he responded, "Hello!" It was 12:55 in the afternoon, and he was on his way to his one o'clock quarterly address. If I ever wrote a Little Golden Book, this moment would be the magical ending.

BIOGRAPHY

Lilian Peña is an Account Executive in Sales and Marketing for ABC7/KGO-TV, owned by The Walt Disney Company, and is on the diversity and inclusion team of the ABC owned Television Stations Group.

She is a philanthropist within the Latino Community Foundation, within a network which has granted $2 million in five years to Latino-based Bay Area nonprofits across the state.

Lilian is on the Bay Area Border Relief team, is an Advisory Board Member of Silicon Valley Latino, and recently joined Hispanic Star. She has a Bachelor of Arts in broadcast television and radio from San Francisco State University.

BE RELENTLESS

MARIA PIASTRE

"I am a fierce believer that women in leadership have a responsibility to improve gender dynamics for future generations."

Behind the beauty of precious metals, there is an environment of furnaces, molten metal, mills, wet chemistry…not necessarily the place you would expect to be managed by a woman, but I am that woman: Maria Piastre. I am an immigrant from Colombia, and this is my story.

Fifteen years ago, I got a job at Metallix in inside sales for Latin America. In my mid-twenties, as a young wife and mother with a thick Spanish accent, it never crossed my mind that becoming president of the company was in my future. Allow me to share how it happened personally, and professionally.

First, you ought to be relentless. Don't allow anyone to impose any roles on you. With the high cost of childcare, not having close relatives nearby, and having the financial support of my husband, many questioned my decision to work instead of staying at home with my child. Rather than seeing my husband's support as the opportunity not to work, I saw it as the opportunity to build my career. Besides, my parents are teachers, and I truly believe in the benefits that children gain from structured, early childhood education.

Ladies, please understand that building your independence is imperative. This may sound harsh when you are a young mother but believe me YOU are the priority; that's the only way you'll be truly able to take care of your loved ones.

I'm still married, but you must always have the choice to be where you want to be, not where you need to be. Independence is the real wealth in life.

Second, you ought to be relentless. At work, and more so in a squarely male- dominated industry, I knew I had to work doubly hard to be taken into account. But working hard alone will not get you noticed. If you want to be considered for a bigger job, say it. Raise your hand, find a mentor, and never stop learning. Become the expert at what you do. Read, be informed, be engaged, and embrace who you are. When I first started, I struggled with my accent; I thought I sounded dumb, and this prevented me from fully participating and speaking out. If you are going through this, please allow me to save you some useless anxiety: you are who you are, and that's great. Embrace it, make it your brand, take advantage of being different and thus you will be unforgettable.

Fast forward to 2020 and I am now the president of Metallix Refining. Under my leadership we have expanded our global reach by establishing locations in Europe and Asia. We have also built the most advanced precious metals laboratory in the country, obtained ISO 14000 certification, and continued to expand and improve our processes on a daily basis while instituting policies such as 100 percent paid maternity leave and investing in real and tangible strategies to eliminate the gender gap within our company. I am a fierce believer that women in leadership have a responsibility to improve gender dynamics for future generations.

BIOGRAPHY

Maria Piastre is President of Metallix Refining Inc., a global precious metals recycling company. After being promoted to President of Metallix in 2017, she became one of the few young women, and possibly the only Latinx in an executive role in the precious metals industry. Be relentless.

AN ARCHITECTS PURPOSEFUL JOURNEY

ALICIA PONCE-NUÑEZ

"Every experience is a building block to your chosen path."

As an architect, I believe that every human being should have access to a space that brings them joy. Architecture has the power to provide this through shapes, patterns, and colors. My mission is to build healthy environments that use little to no fossil fuels which helps to combat climate change. Now more than ever, I believe in what I do.

At six years old, I knew I wanted to be an architect. My connection with nature and love of buildings fed my curiosity to pursue this dream and explore what brings joy to a person in a space. Growing up, I happily immersed myself in nature on our visits to Michoacán. As a daughter of Mexican immigrants, I am eternally thankful to my parents. They taught me the meaning of hard work, resilience, and getting the job done.

When I applied for college, I met with my counselor and

"trusted advisor." His only advice was that I attend community college "because the university would be too challenging" for me. Even though I had the grades that proved I could succeed, I didn't get his support. Luckily, my English teacher Mr. Johnson believed in me. His support was key in my attending the University of Illinois' architecture school. That lack of support was one of many instances that would remind me of the Mexican proverb, "They wanted to bury us, they didn't know we were seeds." I believed my dream was the seed which I had to nourish and protect no matter what others tried to say to discourage me.

Several years into my career I was hired by a firm to lead sustainability efforts. Unfortunately, most of my daily tasks were porch repair drawings to bring them up to code. It was work, but it was not what I was promised, nor what inspired me to go to work daily. I was laid off shortly after and although it hurt when it happened, it was the timely kick in the pants I needed. Little did I know that the residential bubble was about to burst across the nation. Before parting, my friend said to me, "Alicia, remember, anything is possible!"

Instantly, I remembered the single client that requested sustainable design services and took the contact information with me. I didn't have a plan, but I had my purpose. Soon after making the call, I founded my firm APMonarch and officially started working on sustainable building projects.

Being a Latina in a white, male-dominated industry has its share of experiences, from meeting lifelong mentors who give you wings, to disappointingly being caught in the #metoo movement.

Either way, every experience is a building block to a chosen path.

Thirteen years in business has given me the privilege to collaborate with many others building toward a more sustainable future. Starting a business was never on my radar, but now I'm an entrepreneur on a mission.

BIOGRAPHY

Alicia Ponce-Nuñez is the founder and principal of APMonarch, an architecture firm with an expertise in sustainable design. Considered as pollinators of the built environment, Alicia has led her team to build radically better buildings.

APMonarch's notable projects include The Field Museum, Midway International Airport, University of Chicago, and Exelon. An alumnus of the University of Illinois at Urbana-Champaign, Alicia is proud to be in the 1 percent of Latina licensed architects in the United States and 20 percent who are female.

She is happily married to Cesar, and they have two kids that keep her inspired and motivated daily.

UNLEASHING YOUR MAGIC WITHIN

TATIANA QUAIFE

"If you're always trying to be normal, you will never know how amazing you can be." - Maya Angelou

Growing up in corporate America as a Latina, a woman of color, hasn't always been easy…

For context, I was born and raised in Brazil and since I was a little girl, I dreamed of becoming a president/CEO of a multinational company. I am not sure why… I think other kids have much more exciting dreams like being an astronaut, a firefighter, or a rock-star but for some reason this was my dream… I would wear my mom's high-heels and carry my dad's briefcase around the house, pretending I was a businesswoman.

The amazing thing is that my parents always told me that I could do and be anything I wanted to be… that I should dream big and reach for the stars… so I did!

Even though Brazil is a very sexist country, my dad believed the world was going to be female... that it would be led by women, so he helped me to step up and get ready... he taught me about leadership, business, and mindset, and encouraged me to keep going.

All the decisions and choices I have made in my life have been helping me get one step closer to my dream of becoming a senior executive, including moving to the U.S. to go to college and starting my career in corporate America.

My first job after undergrad was in a manufacturing plant in the middle of rural Indiana. Every day at work I would look around and notice that I was the only woman and the only person of color in the room.

I didn't see anyone that looked like me in higher executive positions, and that started to really shake my confidence. I also realized I had a different accent, darker skin and hair, and I behaved differently with my loud, bold, and passionate personality.

I learned, perhaps via unspoken words, that to grow in corporate America, I couldn't really be "me." So, I slowly started to adapt. I looked around and tried to emulate and assimilate.

In many ways this "fitting in" approach seemed to be quite effective... I was performing well, moving up the ladder and I was very proud of that. But after a while, I realized that I couldn't be truly happy and fulfilled unless I could be my true self.

So, over the past few years, I have been going through a deep inner journey to heal my wounds, rebuild my confidence, let go of limiting beliefs, and (re)discover my authentic Latina power. I have read many books, attended workshops, and invested back in myself so that I could turn my inner light back on. I've realized that like

Maya Angelou says, "if you're always trying to be normal, you will never know how amazing you can be."

I am now proud of who I really am. Of all of me. I am bringing my full Latina authentic self to work, and my career has taken off because I am no longer holding myself back... I have unleashed my magic within!

BIOGRAPHY

Tatiana Quaife is a Latina executive with more than 10 years of leadership experience at two top companies – The Walt Disney Company and Procter & Gamble.

Her journey of moving to a different country all by herself to follow her dreams and "growing up" in corporate America as a woman of color had many bumps along the way but she learned a lot.

She is now on a mission to change the face of corporate America while helping other Hispanic leaders rise, because deep down she doesn't want her daughter to still see graphs and statistics showing how underrepresented Hispanics are.

AMERICAN DREAMING

SANDRA RAMOS GARCIA

"Immigrants can contribute so much, if we are just given the opportunity."

My oldest memory starts at a safe house. The man holding me asked, "Where is the mother of this child?" My mom comes up quickly and takes me into her arms. She was drenched, and all I could say was, "Eww, you're wet!" Little did I know of the terror she just faced running in the rain, crossing a highway into the U.S. illegally. I'm now much more aware of the sacrifices my parents made by leaving their entire lives and families behind in search of a better future for our family.

Ours is the story of many immigrants in search of the American Dream. My parents did not take this new opportunity lightly and got to work on making their dream a reality. I grew up in Inglewood, California, in a small, two-bedroom home. It was a humble upbringing as my parents couldn't afford the entire rent, so my whole family, all five of us, shared a single room, while the other room was rented out.

My parents did their best to ensure our basic needs were met, but they also understood that an education would afford their children a better future and placed great emphasis on it. We all did our part. My parents worked extremely hard, my mother became very resourceful, and all of us kids did the best we could in school. A move to Colorado provided my family with more opportunities and home ownership.

Of course, there were mistakes made, falling into the wrong crowd during a few rebellious teen years; but even as one of us faltered, we stuck together, and provided support and encouragement to each other.

I learned quickly that no one would be advocating for my siblings and I in school, and my parents were working really hard, so I eventually took on that role. Although I struggled through the first years of high school and had a very bad GPA, my stubbornness and refusal to take no for an answer got me into college.

Fast forward a few years and I graduated with my degree in architecture, and a few years later with an MBA. It was such a proud moment that not only was my dream realized, but also that of my parents. I am beyond grateful to my parents who instilled an ethic of hard work, perseverance, grit, and not giving up.

Along the way, my parents also didn't give up. After starting their own small business, in which all the kids helped, they were even able to pay for all their children's college educations. We are the epitome of the American dream. Immigrants can contribute so much, if we are just given the opportunity, and sometimes, we have to create those chances ourselves.

In gratitude for my good fortune, I volunteer with several organizations to help out in my community. I hope our stories reflect the true nature of our culture; a culture of hard working and loving families, some still in search of the American Dream.

BIOGRAPHY

By day, Sandra Ramos is a dedicated project manager for the University of Colorado where she pursues a career that fulfills her passion for planning, strategy, execution, and leadership.

By night, she is passionate about helping others in her community, which has led her to being involved with several nonprofits, whether as a meal server at the Denver Rescue Mission, swinging a hammer with Habitat for Humanity, or as a board member for the Denver Chapter of Prospanica, and BCC Evolution.

FEELING OUT OF PLACE

ALBERTO RIVERON

"If not now, when?"

As a little boy, on a Freedom Flight, I never thought I would grow up to become the NFL's first Hispanic referee. In January of 1966, I was five years old when my mom made the decision to emigrate from Cuba to Miami, to pursue a better future for us both. In retrospect, it was a very scary decision…to leave everything you know behind and only look forward, but she did it for us.

I don't remember much about living in Cuba, but I do know that I never truly felt out of place in Miami. A city that is rich in Hispanic flavor and history quickly became my home and what I knew. Many kids in my neighborhood played soccer during their free time.

Soccer wasn't for me. For whatever reason, I was drawn to football. There was just something about the game that made me fall in love at a young age. My mom called it *"el juego de los empujones"* or "the game of pushing". Football is what I was (and still am) truly passionate about, every aspect of the game.

My interest in officiating peaked in the late 70's when I was invited to attend a football officiating clinic. Shortly after training, I began officiating Pop Warner football games, taking as many as six on any given day. I couldn't get enough. I eventually added Friday night high school football games to my resume. I loved being out there under the lights each week. It was almost like an adrenaline rush that I kept going after. I wanted to continue to refine my craft. I didn't know how far I could go with officiating, but I was determined to find out.

Landing a job in college officiating wasn't easy, but by seizing the opportunities in front of me, I did get to that level. I spent the majority of my college officiating career in the Big East and Conference USA, mostly as a referee. In 2002, I was approached to officiate for NFL Europe and then in 2004, I was hired as an NFL side judge. That's when I became the first Hispanic to officiate in the NFL.

Eventually, I saw a promotion to crew chief in 2008. I was a crew chief until my retirement after the 2012 season and then I transitioned to the league office. Now, I currently serve as the Senior Vice President of Officiating in the football operations department.

I'm passionate about my job because I love football. I saw a rise in my career because of my hard work and my determination for having the best product on the field. One of the NFL's core values is integrity, and I resonate closely with that. Football is at its best when everyone shares a common goal.

The road throughout my life was never easy and sometimes it seemed extremely long. I found success in seizing opportunities...

you should never let an opportunity pass you by. Always remind yourself, if not now, when?

BIOGRAPHY

Alberto Riveron, a member of the NFL's Officiating Department since 2013 and a nine-year veteran NFL game official, is the NFL Senior Vice President of Officiating.

A native of Cuba, Riveron moved to Miami at age five with his family and developed a passion for the game. He began as an official in local youth leagues in 1977, made his collegiate officiating debut in 1990 before joining the NFL officiating ranks in 2004.

In 2008, Riveron was promoted to referee, earning the distinction as the NFL's first Hispanic referee. Riveron came off the field following the 2012 season to join the league office.

PERSEVERANCE IN THE FACE OF ADVERSITY

DIANA RODRIGUEZ-ZABA

"Be humble, eliminate barriers, be fearless, and take risks."

At age 24, I was feeling very accomplished, I had graduated college, I owned a lot of real estate, and was making good money. Then one day I received a lay-off notice. Immediately I knew I had to start a business; filing for unemployment was frowned upon by my parents and being unemployed was never an option. I needed a miracle, fast!

2008 was one of the worst years for startups, but I had no choice. No one was hiring. Businesses were closing. My fiancé, now husband, was a union carpenter who was also getting laid off. I had many years of franchising experience and real estate investing, as well as successfully rehabbing several properties. My fiancé and I combined our skills, bought our franchise and launched ServiceMaster Restoration by Zaba. With my business background, we decided I would be the face of the company.

When I first launched my business, women were underrepresented in the field. As the face of my company, I needed to be experienced, knowledgeable, and in charge of decision-making. Having my voice heard was a little challenging in this field and I felt like I was not going to fulfill my purpose.

Growing up, my father was, and still is, my rock. With only an elementary school education, he taught me all my important life lessons. He worked seven days a week providing for my mom and my three brothers. He taught me everything, from how to change a tire to how to install a toilet. He tried his hand at entrepreneurship, but things didn't work out.

As a Mexican man and father, he instilled in me that I should always be treated as an equal. I saw how deeply he respected my mother and how much he valued her as a person. He also taught me to be humble, eliminate barriers, be fearless, and take risks. He always said success was not going to be easy.

As I got to know the business better, I started writing about women in the male-dominated restoration industry. I covered topics like breaking down barriers and empowering women on the job. Over the years, my views gained credibility. It was so satisfying to see more and more women acknowledged in my field.

I want to open doors for other women in this male-dominated industry, so I mentor them. The individuals I hire have so much potential. I am grateful to provide them with the opportunity to improve and advance.

Recently the entire world was shaken by the COVID-19 pandemic. I take every opportunity to learn new lessons and expand my business. I expanded our specialty cleaning division and started providing COVID-19 cleanings to affected businesses, as well as vandalism clean-ups for businesses affected by the current riots.

Nothing has been easy, but I know it was my feistiness that got me through all these years of hard work, and now I see how all of that has come together.

BIOGRAPHY

Diana Rodriguez-Zaba is the president of ServiceMaster Restoration by Zaba, a woman and minority-owned cleaning and restoration company in Chicago and suburbs.

Diana stands as a pillar of strength for her staff, clients, family, and community. In the middle of the 2008 recession, she launched two ServiceMaster brands.

Her business has grown to become one of Illinois' most successful franchises, proudly serving one of the largest territories around Chicago.

TIME TRAVELLING IN NEW YORK

MARIALOREN RODRIGUEZ

"I realized that bravely broadcasting my culture was the right path to being the winner 'la ganadora'."

It was an electrifying feeling. I have spun the immigrant wheel of fortune with my very own elbow grease. Yes, I'm standing here. Yes, me, a young Hispanic woman standing upright alongside 23 young American men bearing a close resemblance to the Olympic Games ceremony.

Twelve arduous weeks, 18 hours per day of self-learning how to code, having no previous technological background, and I am now being handed a certificate that says "Java Performance Engineer." It is my greatest achievement in education and resilience.

There's no way in the world I am quitting this, is what I whispered to myself every night that I stayed up until three o'clock in the morning writing code. I am a person who chases my dreams to the finish line. Only three months earlier I was achieving something else entirely different, *el sueño Americano*, the New York dream.

I was briskly marching around the corner of 5th Avenue and 45th Street in Manhattan, flowing with the crowd. I was interning in a high fashion studio for a celebrity makeup guru to complete my bachelor's in business and arts. Helping manage the studio placed me directly in high rise magazine buildings, public relations firms, and fashion shows on a daily basis.

With the glamorous work life came an unsophisticated hour and a half commute from a very small, very expensive, ugly apartment, but on the daily ferry ride I saluted the Statue of Liberty.

New Jersey's unofficial slogan is "I love New York" and so was mine. I was 16 when I was given invitations to New York by top casting agents, showcasing my public speaking, singing, and acting at major talent expos. Latinos truly need representation in the shows that have influence in our culture and our children.

This conference hallway was crammed with 15-year-old girls and their moms. At the double doors they placed a soda commercial script in my hands. In order to win I had to stand out from the 1,200 gifted actors and singers in the crowd. I pretended to sip on a fizzy drink and planted my feet in front of the mic. At the end of my commercial I inserted, *"Es deliciosa!"* I won.

Next I was awarded first place for magazine cover modeling thanks to my multicultural star-like Hispanic look. I realized that bravely broadcasting my culture was the right path to being the winner *"la ganadora"*. 10 years before I had voyaged to the United States, who would've known the struggles and shining opportunities to come.

Just after arriving in the United States, at only 7 years old,

I was chosen out of dozens to sing "The Star-Spangled Banner" at a Cincinnati Reds baseball game. The roaring crowd became silent as I walked to the middle of the field, with the lyrics of the National Anthem floating in my head. My dad couldn't believe he was standing right next to the players. I gazed up captivated by the towering jumbotron TV, showing my shining smile and the bright waving flag together. I had journeyed to the US only four months earlier and there I was, standing firm as the new face of the great American dream.

BIOGRAPHY

MariaLoren Rodriguez is a Full-Stack Software Developer in the Maryland region. She is an American-Venezuelan who moved to the U.S. and was labeled as a gifted child when she was six years old.

She became perfectly bilingual after three months when she was removed from her ESL classes by her teachers. She is also multi-talented in areas outside of software like business, fashion, theater, singing, and drawing.

Maria is passionate about teaching digital skills to Hispanic youth, she is enthusiastic to create more content with her talents that support inclusion and equal opportunities in technology in the U.S.

BLOSSOMING TASTE BUDS

MONIQUE RODRIGUEZ

"Life begins at the end of your comfort zone."

When I was a little girl in El Paso, Texas, I enjoyed rummaging through my mom's spice rack. I'd start by unscrewing the spice cap, closing my eyes, and allowing the scents to transport me. My imagination would run wild. I never understood why I was so enamored by this sensory frolic that took me to faraway places. I guess my family was right; I was a "dreamer."

The magic was in those bottles. "Comino" and "canela" for example, staple spices in my house, transported me to my grandmother's Mexican kitchen. To this day, cumin and cinnamon conjure emotions of comfort, love, and deep family bonds.

As I became active in my own kitchen, my love for food and cooking began to grow. The smells of spices continued to inspire me to dream, which was all I could do at the time. As a single mom raising two children in New York City and working full-time, it was a stretch just to cook for family and friends.

That didn't stop me from continuing to daydream about

owning my own food-related business someday. I started saving money in my "someday" fund with the intention of using it on something special...one day! I saved and saved and finally after saving for years, something "special" presented itself.

After a food photography retreat I attended, I became motivated by the impact of beautiful photos and the emotions they could evoke in others who love cooking and spice, just like me. The retreat gave me the confidence I needed to start my own food blog.

At that time, I started creating spice kits for friends to arouse their curiosity about my recipes. The feedback was incredible! I then searched for interesting glass jars that would add a little extra pizzazz to my blends. After searching far and wide, I stumbled across a small provisions company with the exact bottle I had in mind - "Old Salt Merchants." I sent them a note and asked them if they could share their bottle source. It was proprietary, but they had extras to sell. So, I placed an order.

Little did I know that order would lead me to a new food adventure. Three weeks later, the owners of Old Salt Merchants, John and Irene, sent me a note telling me they had been thinking about selling their business. They loved my blog and really wanted someone who was passionate about food to take over their spice business.

After some deep soul searching and contemplating whether my "someday" had arrived, I decided to take a chance on dreams and serendipity. After all, these two people who I barely knew just gave me the biggest "someday" opportunity of my life! I bought the business in August 2018 and what an incredible journey it has been so far. Life truly begins at the end of your comfort zone!

Not only did the smells of spices inspire me to dream, they sent me on a journey that inspired those dreams to blossom!

BIOGRAPHY

Monique Rodriguez is the owner of Old Salt Merchants. Old Salt Merchants is a woman-owned and operated provisions company born in the Victorian Seaport of Port Townsend, Washington, and currently anchored in Berkeley, California. It is a boutique company motivated by its passion for food and enduring love of adventure. Its mission is to help expand customer palates by sourcing the finest salts, sugars, and teas that are bold and irresistibly unique. Be Salty. Be Sweet. Be Spicy.

MY JOURNEY FROM COOKIE CONSUMER TO TECH FOUNDER

CAROLYN RODZ

"Every business starts small, but from those tiny seeds grows global solutions, and it's high time we unlock that potential."

My childhood summers were largely spent in Bolivia, a mixture of carefree days with my cousins and tagalong excursions with my grandmother, our family's matriarch and the fearless entrepreneur at the helm of the country's largest cookie and bread factory.

When it came time to choose my own career, those summers in Bolivia put international development high on my list. I knew I needed to play a role in building opportunities for those who weren't born with it, so I shadowed an executive at the World Bank in Bolivia as he visited remote villages, where I witnessed extreme wealth disparity.

We spent days in the field, helping indigenous communities navigate food deserts, water shortages, and a lack of education; at the same time I watched my grandmother educate and fund these same populations through her company's employee support programs. She was fueling a lifestyle for our family while empowering employees and their families -- and it all happened through simple commerce.

My career evolved through a hodge-podge of experiences, as I countered a fat investment banking salary with the creativity of a retail business. I closed a business and sold a business, but through it all, I remain convinced that entrepreneurship is the key to sustainable, systemic change. It creates a win-win scenario for both risk-taker (the entrepreneur), and supporter (employees, communities, and customers).

Unfortunately, entrepreneurship is a winding, messy, and obstacle-ridden path, and there isn't a clear guide to help small business owners navigate it. The ones who succeed are almost exclusively those who start with a full toolkit, including money, advisors, education, and exposure to best practices.

If I was experiencing these barriers as a college-educated, middle-class Latina entrepreneur in the fourth largest city in the most developed country in the world, what were others experiencing as they started companies?

Resources were held captive in tight-knit circles, affectionately referred to as "supernodes" among the Silicon Valley elite. In spite of a decades-long discussion around diversity and inclusion, the static numbers don't lie: our current systems don't work for most aspirational business owners.

So, like any entrepreneur, I went back to the drawing board: how could we arm every entrepreneur with the toolkit they needed? And more importantly, what do they need? Research quickly proved the solution isn't a one-size-fits-all approach.

An owner's personal profile and the type of business they are trying to grow largely influence the solutions that work. Yet the support for them was very linear: no matter who you are or where you come from, there was a single recommended path. In order to solve the inequities of entrepreneurship, and by extension bring more innovative solutions to our world's most pressing problems, we need systemic change that accounts for the unique circumstances of single business owners, and we need to implement this change at scale.

Technology, and most importantly, smart, personalized technology, is key. Every business starts small, but from those tiny seeds grows global solutions, and it's high time we unlock that potential.

And so it goes that I, a self-diagnosed cookie addict with deep roots in La Paz, Bolivia, came to run a tech company.

BIOGRAPHY

Carolyn Rodz is the founder and CEO of Hello Alice, a free, predictive technology that helps entrepreneurs forge their unique path to starting and growing a business, based on their unique profile.

Hello Alice offers grants, tools, mentorship, and networks to every business owner with a big vision. Through partnerships with governments and national organizations prioritizing the needs of diverse entrepreneurs, Carolyn advocates for the New Majority small business owner, and believes data is the path for sustainable, systemic change.

STEPPING UP TO PAY IT FORWARD

WANDA RONQUILLO

"Success isn't just handed."

My professional passion became one of "spreading success so that success can spread." It was one of taking personal responsibility to ensure that the path for others was open, clear, and safe to follow. It was about ensuring the success of others, taking responsibility for others, making myself available to others, guiding others, and enabling others with the right tools and skills.

My objective and message is to ensure that the next generation could avoid the bumps and bruises as they navigated along their own path and took responsibility for others as well. That was all I asked of them. When I was taking time out for my mentees and students at the university and K-12 levels, it was all about inspiring, showing them what could be, letting go of any fear, value working with a sense of urgency, and learning to problem solve, challenge themselves, and maintain a work/life balance.

As the only daughter with five brothers, my parents made sure I was protected, restricted, and understood the value of respect and honor. Extracurricular activities in middle and high school became my way "out." Ultimately, good grades and excelling in math were what opened up those precious doors to my next chapter.

Scholarships followed and I pursued a teaching degree in math in spite of my counselor encouraging me "to just get married." She did not believe I had what it took to get through college, even though I pushed for our high school to offer a calculus class, was senior class president, and was a member of the top 10 percent. To this day, I credit my high school math teacher and the local League of United Latin American Citizens (LULAC) chapter for having confidence in me to create success.

I did get married after my first year in college and I did complete my education with a bachelor's degree in business administration and followed up with an MBA and professional certifications in project management. I will say that my biggest regret was not pursuing an engineering degree when I had the chance early in my career. It would have taken just one more semester. Oh, how I wished someone would have questioned what I was doing. I needed a mentor.

I ultimately made it happen by enrolling in IBM's New Programming Training Program, and that is how I became a software engineer for the next 14 years. IBM all along provided the support, the education, and the tools. It was just up to me to take advantage of the offerings, invest the time, and produce results.

In 1997-98, IBM announced the creation of Diversity Network Groups. By springing into action, I became one of IBM's trailblazers in "paying it forward" to my community within IBM and more importantly, the external Latinx community. That type of volunteering and leadership gave me and my team access to IBM 's community grants for the sake of "spreading success" to the underserved. Within IBM, I also helped connect other network groups across IBM from coast to coast. I make sure that individuals worthy of recognition stand out. Needless to say, I am for those who are "spreading success".

My husband Dave and I became dual career IBMer's for over three decades. Although I am referred to as "Mama SHPE" in the Society of Hispanic Professional Engineers, our priorities remained with our two sons. I believe success isn't just handed to you. For the Latinx community, it is created through results.

The expectations are exponentially higher for our community. Therefore, one has to believe in hard work paying off. Good devoted mentors are few and far between which is why I advocate for taking responsibility for spreading success to others and for others.

BIOGRAPHY

Wanda Ronquillo is a senior resolution technical manager in the IBM Storage Project Office supporting Spectrum and Data Protection & Replication product critical situations.

She was in management for 10 years maintaining positions in Storage Tape, Disk, network- attached storage (NAS), and SAN, and was a software engineer for 14 years.

She holds an executive MBA, MSC from George Washington University in project management, a BSBA, and an active PMP certification from the Project Management Institute (PMI) New York City and from Stanford University.

Wanda has been recognized by a Women of Color "All Star Technologist" and was the recipient of the 2008 Society of Hispanic Professional Engineers (SHPE) Junipero Serra Award and the 2018 Jaime Oaxaca Award, SHPE's highest honor.

SEEING RACISM THROUGH THE EYES OF LOVE AND COMPASSION

ADRIANA ROSALES

"Write as if your life depends on it, share like it makes a difference, and speak like God is listening."

In 1989, I was a 14-year-old kid working my first job at the Capitola Mall in Santa Cruz County. I couldn't believe it– finally I didn't have to work picking raspberries with my dad during the hot summers. It's not like I didn't like working in the fields with my dad; it was that in high school, the white kids I knew made reference to how awful it was.

So, throughout the years, I learned to "assimilate" into a culture that has yet to see me as part of America. I also learned to heal my wounds that were due to racism and resentment through love and compassion.

I grew up in Watsonville, California. Watsonville is primarily Latino and the amount of gang activity and violence I saw growing up would be unheard of in Aptos, a small city just twenty minutes away. Nevertheless, for high school I was shipped to Aptos High, an all-white school. There, I learned there was a great big world I'd never interacted with.

Racial slurs on the bathroom walls and being called all sorts of crazy names was commonplace. Finding a happy medium between being a "real" Latina and a "real" American was my internal ruckus at the time because I didn't know I could be both.

Most of the name calling were words I had never heard before, so I'd go to the library to look them up. To my dismay they were disparaging, but I adjusted. What else could I do? Fight an entire population of teenagers brought up to believe I was stupid and a threat because of my *"Latinidad"*?

The way I saw it at the time, I was quite civil. I would show up to school with a white t-shirt that read "Stop Racism." I marked the t-shirt up with a sharpie and then I'd walk around during lunch break so everyone could read it.

This was in the late 80s so, you can image people thought I was super weird. Now I just laugh, because not much has changed. Still we must write as if your life depends on it, share like it makes a difference, and speak like God is listening.

After high school, I moved on and became a rather well-adjusted, contributing citizen just like the American system wanted me to, but not after learning some important lessons. While peeling back the layers of my life story I found this to be true; we cannot reciprocate ignorance with ignorance. The world does not operate like this, at least not in my dimension.

The United States of America is a relatively young country compared to other countries. Its traditions and its very own national ethical code of conduct is just now emerging and being redefined by a younger generation. Other countries have thousands of years of wisdom to decipher and learn from, not us. Not much has changed since high school in this country, however ***I have changed***, and this makes all the difference in the world and ***how I see the world.***

BIOGRAPHY

Adriana Rosales is a seven-time author, featured as one of Forbes expert panelists and a Forbes Coach Council member. She is a John Maxwell Certified Speaker, and a HeartMath® Coach. Her books have been translated into several languages. She continues to inspire women to write their personal stories in her yearly Latinas 100 project.

An accomplished military veteran, she brings her background and years of experience navigating the corporate ladder to the front lines in her book, *Corporate Code, A Bottom-Up Perspective on Great Leadership.* Her leadership philosophy revolves around four leadership pillars trust, courage, compassion, and service.

EVERY SECOND OF OUR LIVES

ADRIANA ROZO-ANGULO

"My character is only the result of the experiences, changes, and trials I encountered during the years, and how I decided to react at every second of my life."

Who is Adriana? I asked my husband and his response did not surprise me; however, it made me think on how I can use the perception that people have of me to encourage them. "Adriana is not the typical woman or mom. She is not the kind of woman that will volunteer to bake a pie to raise funds for a school. Instead, Adriana will run a Sparta race for a cause, or will go on a mission trip to help communities rebuild their homes."

I am a passionate person with the ability to embrace change and look for efficiencies at any circumstance. My faith made me a fearless and strong person. My character is only the result of the experiences, changes, and trials I encountered during the years, and how I decided to react at every second of my life.

My life has been filled by constant changes. My parents

divorced when I was nine years old; it was a difficult time, but my mom's strong character taught me that we need to have the courage to leave toxic situations and work hard for our dreams, even if our entire social circle says no.

I had a good life, full of good mentors and rich in experiences. For nine years, I was part of the Scouts in Bogota, Colombia, and learned the importance of integrity, service, and survival skills. Those years connected me with nature and the adrenaline that a good adventure can bring.

When I was in college, the biggest change of my life took place; my mom accepted a job in Puerto Rico. We left everything--our house, our friends, our lifestyle. It was a point of no return. Shortly afterwards, we moved to New Jersey without knowing English. I had to learn English at the same time I was taking college classes.

When I started working in corporate America, like many women, I had to prove myself and demonstrate that I was able to perform successfully and bring good ideas. On a couple of occasions, I was told that I could not be in charge because the people that were working for me were either men or American women.

Yes, they said that to my face. For a time, I struggled with this, and I felt insecure and started looking at my flaws, my accent, and everything that could validate their statement. I believe that those phases of insecurity are only the prologue and are intended to be short.

For me, it was the phase where I obtained the tools that developed my character. I learned how to create strategies, multitask, and more importantly, believe in myself. During the journey, my strategy changed as I was achieving my goals and climbing the ladder, while I was raising my kids.

Today, I am thankful for my life and moreover for the journey. It went exactly how God planned for me to become the person I am today. I am re-launching my company and pursuing bigger dreams.

BIOGRAPHY

Adriana Rozo-Angulo was born in Bogota, Colombia, and moved to this country when she was 18 years old. She has two kids, Sebastian, 21 years old, and, Matthew, 15 years old. She lives in Scotch Plains, New Jersey.

Adriana is a director of operations with 20 years of experience in operations and quality in the pharmaceutical, packaging, and medical devices industries and a Hispanic Star New Jersey Hub Leader. Adriana and her husband, Miguel Angulo, are the founders of MAS Connections, a business consulting company established in 2011.

A TALE OF TWO CONFERENCES

OMAR RUIZ

"There is a great responsibility to succeed."

"Hi, Omar Ruiz, welcome."

I had no idea one simple, friendly greeting would highlight the memories of a weekend 12 years ago that provided such long-lasting motivation and inspiration for my career. Back in 2008, while working as a weekend sports anchor at the NBC affiliate in Columbus, Ohio, our station, industry, and country were struggling financially because of the economic recession.

So much so, we weren't going to attend the Big Ten football media days--an important event on our work calendar, where all the coaches, select players, and media members who cover the conference, congregate for interviews and other events to generate excitement for the upcoming season.

In Columbus, college football--specifically, Ohio State football--is king, so I volunteered to travel to Chicago to cover the event on my dime because I said I'd be there anyway that weekend to attend another conference, the UNITY journalists convention in Chicago.

That conference, as its title suggests, united the major organizations supporting journalists of color, the National Association of Black Journalists, the National Association of Hispanic Journalists, the Asian-American Journalists Association, and the Native American Journalists Association.

I had never attended an industry-related developmental or educational conference and was curious to see what one of these networking events was all about. Turns out, I could not have had a better experience. I met so many amazingly talented people from all over the country, many of whom looked like me, had names that sounded like mine, and shared my same career aspirations.

As for that friendly greeting I first told you about, we have to go back to the Big Ten media days. I didn't know the woman who said hello to me that day but recognized her as a representative of the Big Ten who had helped me check in to pick up my credentials for the conference the day prior.

I asked her how she remembered my name, because we had never met before that quick encounter and there were hundreds of media in town for the event. She explained that she had a grandmother that was of Hispanic descent and my name caught her attention because of the 300 or so people she had checked in, I was the only one with a Hispanic last name."

Whoa! To be the "only one in the room," in a room that big, was certainly shocking, but also inspiring and motivating, especially when juxtaposed with the other conference I was attending that weekend, where there were so many of "us," a-not-so-subtle reminder that we are still fighting for representation.

I take pride and joy in doing my job, and there is a great responsibility to succeed so that we may provide a path for others to come behind us and join us in these rooms, large and small, and better reflect the audiences we serve.

BIOGRAPHY

Based in Los Angeles, Omar Ruiz is currently a news reporter and anchor at the NFL Network, the first Latino sportscaster at the network, as he was, previously, at the NHL Network.

He's a proud Californian, equally proud of his Mexican-American heritage. Omar graduated from San Diego State University, and then earned a master's degree from Syracuse University.

His first full time sportscasting job came in the Monterey/Salinas/Santa Cruz market in Northern California.

GO TO A PRISON AND IT WILL CHANGE YOUR LIFE

CHARLIE RUTH

"You don't know how strong you are until being strong is the only option."

Have you heard, "When the student is ready, the teacher will appear?" I'm the daughter of that phrase. I am Colombian and have learned that education is the key to escape from systematic poverty. My grandparents were farmers. My parents attended college and became entrepreneurs, and I went to Harvard.

Growing up, we had no-frills, but our house was full of love, discipline, and intellectual stimulation. I love learning something new every day, and I am a professional optimist with a passion for solving problems. Every year I got scholarships, from kinder to Universidad de Los Andes. I was studying law and business management when I met the one who was going to give me my fellowship and my work at Harvard University.

While in Boston, I was the program director from *Conectados* al Sur at Berkman Klein Center, and I dedicated my time to making girls and women feel powerful, valuable, and able to reach their greater potential through improving their health and access to education.

In 2017, I quit the Berkman Klein Center, traveled for four months throughout Washington, San Francisco, and Lima, then returned to Bogotá to launch MujeresConDerechos.org, my own social innovation lab to gather outstanding Latin American leaders to empower girls and women who need it most.

My life changed when I visited a prison the first time. Fortunately, I got there as a motivational speaker, and not for the two strongest reasons pushing the 90 percent of women to commit crimes in Latin America: violence and deep poverty. A Colombian is the kind of place where people give up their dignity and eat their dreams every day.

But flowers bloom in adversity. My team and I created the first innovative business program within a Colombian prison. We gave design thinking tools to 250 women and helped them create small businesses in and out of prison. In 2018, I extended my program to the Guadalajara Women's Prison and my model was honored by the United Nations and Rotary International.

The best prize of all has been learning from these amazing women. They have been my teachers of resilience, creativity, and courage. They taught me you don't know how strong you are until being strong is the only option.

They opened my eyes to a problem affecting 1.9 billion women in the world: menstrual poverty. This lack of access to menstrual products is a public health problem that I have begun to solve through the menstrual cup I designed and launched last year.

My product is needed today more than ever. Women deserve access to a safe, ecological, and economic menstrual cup, as well as a better relationship with our bodies and our health. Gender equality requires menstrual equality. My product can open a larger conversation and inspire women to better understand their health. I am returning to the place I am happiest and where I want to build a global company with the aim to help millions of women: Boston.

I invite you to see the world as your own innovation lab. Open your mind and appreciate your life teachers. Take problems as opportunities to find the best of your creative genius. Embrace adversity and trust me; your teachers will arrive the moment you are ready to change the world.

BIOGRAPHY

Charlie Ruth is a social innovator awarded by the United Nations and Rotary International for her contribution empowering thousands of Latin American girls and women.

A TED-Speaker, lawyer, author, and expert developing communities around innovation and women's rights, Charlie is an Alumni Fellow at the Berkman Klein Center for Internet & Society at Harvard University, the director of the Women with Rights Foundation *(www.MujeresConDerechos.org)* and creator of the Powerful Menstrual Cup.

DREAMS COME AND GO, PASSION IS FOREVER!

DOUGLAS SANTIAGO

"How do I engage and exist?"

I was waiting to go home from a two-month hospital stay, recovering for the second time from being nearly dead. A situation I never saw myself in. It was me against the grim reaper. It came in the form of a young temptress, who slithered up my almost-home legs and tried to blind and choke me from envisioning total immortality and earning my second chance.

This may seem a bit heavy, but when I woke up, I felt a void, a memory of when things were better and now I question, *How do I engage and exist before my history catches up?* The lesson is to know and forgive myself, then make the necessary mistakes to change and heal.

I went on a mission looking for relationships and community that would lead me to greatness. Survival became a burning tattoo tracing my challenges. My journey became selfish at times, and I frequently found myself cornered and hopeless, everyday wishing for more positives than my surroundings had to offer. I grew up in several homes with mostly lower-class families and before my eyes opened in the morning, I was already plotting how to escape, see the big city, and become a Hispanic Star.

My star resembled the ones in the sky, untouchable by the withering days. A star that sparkled and lit the most remote heart in the universe. I wanted to never fall and always shine and leave a trail of hope in the brightening dark sky. How could I become triumphant and help the masses? How could I provide for my family and people and get worldly support? My answer: the arts and acting.

I felt my dreams best translated in full color with music, on a stage, saying yes, I can. I looked for a place to color and set myself apart. I pushed through my social and religious storms and shaped my behavior. Along the way I found supportive and inspirational influences from mentors, strangers, and lovers.

I worked on modeling myself for the better of women and men, until eventually I picked myself up. Through art, I feel alive. I celebrate myself. I get that extra push of passion that creates freedom from the construed structures of the world.

To love and know what I do, and walk in my bare warrior feet, rejoicing in the knowledge that today is another day to improve everything around me. To protect my family and neighbors and confirm that goodness leads to greatness and our unique experiences have value. I follow my heart and faith carries me on its back.

BIOGRAPHY

Douglas Santiago boxed his way into the international spotlight in the critically acclaimed Sony Pictures film, *Girlfight.* He then went on to co-star with Leonor Benedetto in the film, Times Up and was cast in the one-man show, *Mambo Mouth.*

His television credits include an Emmy-nominated episode of Law and Order, and a film, A Murder to Die For. Douglas was a member of Subliminal NY on Sire records.

His recent projects include *Only a Glass Inside of Me* and the film, *Southside.* He is currently in production of *Thank You Mr. Douglas and Talk...The Hook.* Douglas Santiago has a Bachelor of Arts degree and is the CEO of ACTN10.

1,000 SANDWICHES

EDGAR SANTIAGO

"While in this life, you must help the less fortunate; if not, you're just wasting your time here."

"Puerto Rico is Destroyed." "Puerto Rico is underwater." "Island-wide Blackout." "No Food, No Water." These were some of the headlines coming out of Puerto Rico days after one of the most powerful hurricanes hit the Caribbean Island in over a century.

Sitting in my office in New York on September 17, 2017, I began my day scrolling through social media, looking for the latest updates on Hurricane Maria's landfall in Puerto Rico.

The images I saw cut straight through me and left me with an empty feeling that I couldn't shake. As I'm watching videos of homes being flooded, towns washed away, people crying for help that never came, rivers of tears began streaming down my face as my heart tore in two.

Finally! After a couple of days with no word from my family, my cousin was able to communicate through social media, posting pictures of the front driveway under two feet of water, and what looked like a river running down their street.

Reaching out to my NY-based family and friends who have family on the island, we all found ourselves helpless and searching for answers--something, anything that would help us heal and make sense of what happened to our beautiful, island homeland.

On October 2, the President of the United States of America visited the devastated island to assure the people of Puerto Rico that help was on the way. After blaming the PR government by saying, "I hate to tell you Puerto Rico, but you've thrown our budget a little out of whack," the President visited a church where he tossed toilet paper and paper towels into the crowd shooting them like basketballs to a crowd.

Undeterred by this attitude, I needed to be proactive to help my people somehow. I believe while in this life, you must help the less fortunate; if not, you're just wasting your time here.

It was around that time I began seeing my goddaughter on social media, volunteering her services with the nonprofit organization, World Central Kitchen. She was cooking and prepping meals to be distributed throughout the island in Ponce, Cayay, Utuado, Humacao, etc.

I volunteered my services and was on the island a month after landfall. Accompanied by a good friend of mine from North Carolina, we both left our families in the States to help "our" families on the Island. Both of us traveled with duffel bags filled with supplies like water, canned food, baby diapers, batteries etc.

Arriving at el Coliseo de Puerto Rico, José Miguel Agrelot (more affectionately known as el Choliseo) we went straight from the airport. We showed up to work, and our first assignment was to clean down the kitchen, wipe counters, mop floors, stack boxes of food, etc. Next, they put us on the sandwich line with hundreds of other volunteers.

The goal was to make 1,000 sandwiches every hour and 1,000 sandwiches per hour were made. When 6,000 sandwiches were prepped in five hours, we all let out a loud cheer.

BIOGRAPHY

Edgar Santiago is an entrepreneur, CEO/owner of a boutique digital marketing company and also writes, directs, and produces his own film/video projects. Edgar was born in the Bronx, NY to Puerto Rican parents and has one younger sibling.

He is married 10 years to the love of his life and is the father of two wonderful children. Edgar volunteers his free time as Ambassador to the Hispanic Star New York Hub.

MI CASA ES TU CASA

NANCY ROSADO-SANTIAGO

"I am a bridge that connects different communities."

I was seven years old when I first started volunteering every Thanksgiving Day, serving meals to the less fortunate of the South Bronx in New York City, and I was eight years old when I started volunteering my weekends to help my religion teacher during CCD classes.

Immaculate Conception Church, affectionately known as the "Cathedral of the South Bronx," has been my second home for as long as I can remember. The Sisters of Christian Charity, The Redemptorist Fathers and the Rogers family welcomed me from the very beginning. So much, in fact, that I have been serving meals on Thanksgiving Day throughout most of my life and was the youngest certified catechist of the Archdiocese of New York at that time.

After I graduated from Immaculate Conception School, and throughout my years at Cardinal Spellman High School and New York University, I continued to go back on Thanksgiving Day and to teach CCD.

This calling to serve my community led me to my career, my passion. Not seeing myself, or anyone that looked like me represented in the media I read, heard, and saw, inspired me to work towards change. No one understands the constant battle of having to justify that Hispanics deserve to be seen, heard, and valued more than someone who is on the front-line vying for campaigns that connect this audience with brands and media channels.

Throughout my advertising and marketing career working at Univision, Latina Magazine, The Wall Street Journal U.S. Hispanic, UnCHin Magazine, Televisa, MundoFox, NY Daily News, Altice USA/a4 media, and to this very day, while at Intersection Co, I remain committed to serve my community and continue with my Thanksgiving Day tradition as well as teaching CCD.

During these unprecedented times, that same place that I return to every Thanksgiving Day and also teach CCD, houses and stores the blessings I have been entrusted with from Procter & Gamble and Matthew: 25, along with Census and voting information.

As Hispanic Star New York Hub Lead, I am fortunate to bring the abundance of these blessings "home" and lead efforts in distributing these donations and sharing this vital information throughout New York City, the boroughs, and Westchester. At the same time, I'm spreading the word of hope and unity via street-level media. It is my personal and professional goal to contribute towards moving our community and culture forward. I am a bridge that connects different communities.

As my mother says, "It is during the most difficult and

challenging times that we see the true heart and face of who we are. Stay committed in giving back and serving your community. The beauty of love and faith will shine through for you to share and be a source of hope and happiness to those who need it most."

BIOGRAPHY

Nancy Rosado-Santiago is the daughter of two immigrants from Ecuador. She is the first U.S.-born citizen of her family and grew up with her parents and brother on 145th Street and Brook Avenue in the Bronx, New York City.

Currently, she works at Intersection, focusing on multicultural advertising and DEI efforts. Nancy has been married for 10 years to her high school confidant, Edgar Santiago, and has two wonderful children, Joaquin Lua and Camila Rosa.

Through much of her life she has been recognized for her community work and outreach. Nancy thanks her parents and brother for her love and commitment to serve the Hispanic community in New York and across the country.

LIVING THE AMERICAN DREAM

NANCY SCOVOTTI

"Surround yourself with people who are going to lift you higher and make the uncomfortable feel like the natural next step."

I am a "Chicana," born in Chicago from 100 percent Mexican parents. I was raised by my single mom who worked two jobs. I vividly remember the bright bedroom lights on my face every morning while she helped me get dressed to go to daycare while it was still dark outside, so she could go to her first job.

After daycare I would go to the babysitter, and she picked me up when it was dark again, after her second shift. Although we had humble beginnings, somehow, she managed to give my two brothers and I an abundance of love in our home (love is her secret). Due to limited means and mindset, achieving the "American Dream" of owning a home was never a thought.

Seventeen years ago, as a young, newly engaged couple, my husband suggested we buy a condominium and my natural response was, "Why not rent?" I was living with my mom and she was renting--that's all I knew. Ironically, I had all the contacts at my fingertips, I just did not know enough to even ask.

A few days later, my boss randomly mentioned there was a foreclosed condominium unit I should see and consider buying. My natural response was, "sure." He was my boss, so of course I said yes. Then, I thought back to one of Richard Branson's quotes, *"If somebody offers you an amazing opportunity but you are not sure you can do it, say YES - then learn how to do it later!"* At that time, I did not realize it was a great opportunity and how it was going to impact my future!

Our next step was finding out if we qualified for a mortgage. Being in the title insurance industry, I already had connections, and sure enough I got the quick answer that it was cheaper to buy than rent. Wow, that was an eye opener!

After learning the buying process and what we could spend, we put in our offer for the condo, but sadly enough, we were outbid. However, buying was now our only option because we were determined to become homeowners. Shortly thereafter, we purchased our very first condo unit.

Five years later, we sold it and doubled our investment. With that, we had our down payment to buy the home we live in now with our kids, in a fantastic school district. Had we rented, we would have had nothing to put towards our purchase.

Fortunately, I was surrounded by people who encouraged and influenced me to have more. My husband always thinks BIG and my manager walked the walk and talked the talk. I knew following his footsteps would lead us in the right direction. Surround yourself with people who are going to lift you higher and make the uncomfortable feel like the natural next step.

As I get older, engage in deeper conversations, and roll in different circles (I call it diversifying), it becomes blatantly obvious that the people you surround yourself with truly matter. Be protective and selective to who you spend most of your time with; it truly makes a huge difference.

BIOGRAPHY

Nancy Scovotti was born in Chicago raised by a hardworking, single Mexican mom. She currently resides in New York with her beautiful family and is the Title Insurance Senior Vice President with The Great American Title Agency.

She has earned a reputation throughout the real estate industry for her efficiency and commitment to customer service.

REPRESENTATION MATTERS IN ALL ASPECTS OF LIFE

KAREN SILES

"Understand the value of representation, giving back through mentoring, and above all learn that despite all odds, only YOU can stop yourself."

"Hey Karen, can I talk to you after class?" asked my ninth-grade biology teacher.

"Yes," I replied. I was so nervous, having just moved to America. I really was not sure if I was in trouble. After class, Mrs. Garcia told me about a summer program and said I would be a good candidate for it. The application was due in two weeks, and I had to discuss it with my parents.

Excited, I talked to my parents, and they decided we could not afford the program. As the oldest of three, I knew that the summer program fees amounted to two months of lunches for our family. I filled out the application anyway but did not submit it since I didn't have my parent's permission.

Surprisingly, we got a call one day from the program director of the Center for Advancement of Hispanics in Science and Engineering Education (CAHSEE) summer program. They told me I had been accepted and I should submit my deposit fee. After translating to my mom, we both looked at each other and explained our situation. We were perplexed as to why they had my application.

It turned out that Mrs. Garcia had applied to the program on my behalf and even wrote a letter of recommendation. The program director of CAHSEE worked with my parents and I to provide the smallest deposit we could afford and find scholarships for me to attend. Little did I know, that this one moment in my life would be the catalyst that would change my entire career and life choices.

I did not know what to expect from the program, but after the first day I realized it would be life changing. There were students from middle and high schools from around the DC metro area, and I was the only one representing mine, Annandale High School in Annandale, Virginia. The program was geared towards Hispanics, featuring college-level math and science courses taught by college students from around the U.S.

The biggest lesson from the four years I attended this program was that representation matters. As an impressionable sophomore, I was astonished by one of the summer course teachers, who was a junior pursuing an electrical engineering degree from the University of South California (USC) and was born and raised in Argentina.

The way she taught science and math made it seem easy. I saw myself in her and wanted to be her. In 2003, I declared my major to be electrical engineering at George Mason University.

I learned some of the best life lessons so far during the

summers of 1999-2002. Thanks to the program, I now understand the value of representation, giving back through mentoring, and above all, learning that despite all odds, only YOU can stop yourself.

Mrs. Garcia was the catalyst to push me into a program that made me aware of how much I could achieve if I worked hard and believed in myself. Fast-forwarding to 2020, I believe in those values even more today, and I work every day to give back and help our youth succeed in all ways that I can, whether through time, treasure, or talent.

BIOGRAPHY

Karen Mariela Siles was born and raised in Cochabamba, Bolivia. Her family migrated to America in 1998, moving to the Northern Virginia area to be close to the Bolivian Community.

In May 2007, she graduated from George Mason University with a bachelor's degree in electrical engineering. She followed her passion to work for the company of her dreams, IBM Corporation.

In July 2007, Karen moved to Austin, Texas, and is currently a Senior Delivery Manager for IBM Cloud Block Storage Services. In May 2019, she obtained an M.S. in Technology Commercialization (MSTC) from the University of Texas-Austin.

SOLVING ELECTRIFYING QUESTIONS THROUGH CROWDSOURCING

DR. GUSTAVO STOLOVITZKY

"Never forget your roots."

I was born in Buenos Aires, Argentina, to a typical middle-class family. My parents were also born there, to immigrant families that left their respective countries to escape poverty and war. They instilled in me a sense of self-confidence and compassion that has accompanied me throughout my life.

When I was six years old an electrifying question obsessed me: if I kept the TV set switched off, would there still be electricity in the two pins of the plug? To investigate the matter, I switched off the TV, separated the plug from the power outlet to expose the plug pins and I touched the two electrodes. I then learned that in fact there is still electricity in the plug, a lesson taught by a 220V electrical kick that I still remember vividly.

This electrifying curiosity was the driving force that led me to pursue a scientific career. Encouragement came early in the fifth grade when an excellent teacher saw something in me and taught me the Cartesian coordinate system. This trust gave me a great sense of accomplishment and an enduring love of science.

Early on in my University years I came to understand that scientific research has a social contract to fulfill. To reach its potential and service society, we as researchers need to take a step back and understand what limits the progress and impact of science.

Some stumbling blocks are technical--those are the ones for which we have trained and are well equipped to address. We are less prepared to understand what limits the societal impact of science. I believe competitiveness and territoriality are among those limits, and that a different approach to research and science is needed, one that is more open and collaborative.

In 2006, I founded the Dialogue for Reverse Engineering Assessment and Methods (DREAM) Challenges. DREAM Challenges merge the notions of collaborative competition and crowdsourcing, enticing the data scientists to verify their methodologies against carefully chosen benchmarks in an open dialogue of ideas and methods called challenges.

Crowdsourced data science challenges can also achieve in months what would take years for groups working independently. Accelerating scientific research through collaboration is therefore an ethical imperative when we are trying to find solutions to societal problems.

With more than 60 challenges organized in key areas of biomedicine such as cancer, neurodegenerative diseases, malaria, and COVID-19, DREAM is arguably one of the most successful scientific competitions in bio-medical research today.

As I learned from my fifth-grade teacher, we need to take time to inspire the new generations that will shape the future of science cognizant of its social responsibility. As the Chair of IBM Exploratory Life Sciences in IBM Research, my duty is that of creating a long-term vision of life sciences at IBM. But that cool job is no less important to me than my work on open and collaborative science and my role and responsibility as a mentor to junior scientists. It's important to never forget your roots.

BIOGRAPHY

Dr. Gustavo Stolovitzky is an Argentine-American scientist, serving as the chair of IBM Research Exploratory Life Science Program. He is also an adjunct associate professor of Biomedical Informatics at Columbia University.

With 80+ issued patents and 150+ published papers, Gustavo is the founder of the Dialogue for Reverse Engineering Assessments and Methods (DREAM). DREAM is an international collaboration whose mission is to promote open science and data sharing to solve pressing biomedical problems faced by society today.

Because of his work on crowdsourcing and nanobiotechnology, Gustavo has been appointed an IBM Fellow, a distinction held by only 114 of 350,000 IBM employees worldwide.

MORE THAN A "FEISTY LATINA"

RAQUEL TAMEZ

"If we're not intentionally including, we're unintentionally excluding."

It feels like a lifetime ago. It feels like yesterday. A few years back, I had a one-on-one meeting with a white male executive. Apparently, he didn't appreciate that I had an opinion. "You're a feisty Latina," he told me. He did not mean this as a compliment.

I kept my cool—barely. But I was stunned. Speechless. For weeks, the comment burned at me like a candle close to the skin. It kept me up at night. In need of advice, I met with one of my cherished mentors.

"Raquel, I'm concerned you'll carry this with you—and not in a good way," he said. "Are you going to lean into being a feisty Latina?"

That's exactly what I did. In May 2017, I joined the Society of Hispanic Professional Engineers (SHPE) as its new CEO. I've probably told the "feisty Latina" story a half dozen times since. It's become part of my narrative.

But there's a fine line between using something as fuel, and letting it define you. I use the feisty Latina episode as fuel to empower not just myself, but my SHPE *familia* my fellow Latinas, and Hispanics across the country. If we're not intentionally including, we're unintentionally excluding.

Heading into 2020, we all felt that empowerment. SHPE had more than 13,000 members. We were nearing 300 chapters across the U.S. We'd launched new, dynamic programs and services. Nearly 10,000 people had attended our 2019 National Convention.

And then the world came to a screeching halt. "Feisty" might inspire a tribe or an organization. It's not enough to weather global upheaval. The COVID-19 crisis has forced SHPE to reimagine and rewire itself—to transition. But we've done more than that. We've transformed. We are transcending to ever-higher heights.

I feel like I've done the same. As a leader, as an advocate for diversity, inclusion and equity, and as a person, SHPE has changed me.

But it's another *familia* that truly shaped me. I'm the daughter of immigrants. My parents came from Mexico for the same reason so many do: to create a better life. They built a house in the Houston barrio. They still live there, in that humble home on Cochran street. Part of me does, too. It will always be home base to me.

My parents showed me the meaning of resourcefulness and resilience. They taught me hard work, honesty, and integrity. These values are why I went to college, then to law school. They're why I took on the challenges I did—and why I eventually came to SHPE.

But I was also a rebel. I pushed back on my parents every

chance I could get. I questioned conventions. In a way, they encouraged it, especially my father, who indulged my boundless curiosity and always made me feel—and still makes me feel—invincible.

My mother taught me to earn respect--and if I didn't get it, to demand it. *"Te tienes que dar tu lugar,"* she would say. You have to stand up for yourself. In their own ways, my parents taught me how to be feisty. And I'm never going to stop. In fact, I'm just getting started.

BIOGRAPHY

Raquel Tamez is CEO of the Society of Hispanic Professional Engineers (SHPE), a national organization focused on empowering the Hispanic community, and creating a powerful network of students and professionals via the promotion of careers in STEM. Since 2017, she has expanded SHPE's national programs and the services it offers to its 13,000-plus members.

Throughout her career and ongoing, Raquel has been honored with various national recognitions and featured in numerous media outlets. She serves on multiple boards and civil task forces to increase diversity and inclusion. Raquel is a native of Texas and currently lives in Washington, DC.

LIFE MAY BE HARD, BUT IT'S WORTH IT!

FERNANDA TAPIA

"Life is so hard, and even when we want to give all that up, we must dust ourselves off and overcome our fears and difficulties."

One year ago, it was two hours before the deadline to complete one of the toughest milestones of my life, and I was at my desk, nervous, and anxious, desperately trying to come up with the words for the last sentences I needed. All I wanted to do was cry. I was trying my best to keep distraction from creeping in and just focus instead. My mind went blank.

I knew what my problem was–stress, anxiety, and exhaustion. I felt defeated and hopeless, and the easy way out was to shut my laptop and just go to sleep, but I knew that meant giving up everything that led me here.

I know firsthand how hard it is to want something and have the doors shut in front of you. I was born in Ecuador and came to live in the United States when I was 14, a tough age. It wasn't easy, the cultural adjustment away from immediate family was difficult.

One of my dreams was to attend an ivy-league school, but I knew it wouldn't be easy. It didn't stop me from taking walks around campus, in awe of the buildings and jealous of the students carrying on with their studies. I admired them–they were lucky, and I told myself that one day, I would be like them.

Life doesn't always give you what you want just because you wish for it. Only with the help of great people can you learn that dreams must be big and complemented by hard work to create magic. It's equally important to accept when things don't work as planned.

When I first applied to Georgetown University, I was rejected. I felt worthless and defeated, but not just because attending there was one of my dreams. It came at a time when my start-up had failed, and life was becoming difficult. Determined to persevere, I continued to push forward because I wanted my education to be with me forever.

The very next year, I was ready and better prepared. I knew exactly what to do and how to do it. That's what my life has been about--big dreams and a relentless work ethic to achieve them.

One year ago, my grandmother's famous words echoed inside my head: *"It doesn't matter what happens in your life, your education will be with you forever."* Suddenly, everything came back into focus, and my drive and inspiration was restored. I slowly pulled myself together and wiped the tears trickling down my cheek. The aperture narrowed, and my big dream came into focus. I wanted to feel proud on graduation day, wearing my cap and gown as a symbol of hard work, dedication, and accomplishment.

Life has taught me to appreciate different experiences and perspectives, and not to be too afraid to ask for help. Don't give up, no matter how hard life may seem. Also, share that experience and perspective with the intent to create positive change. I learned that accomplishments in life cannot be achieved alone–or at least not without the wise words of a loving grandmother who is missed dearly.

BIOGRAPHY

Fernanda Tapia was born in Quito, Ecuador, and moved to Washington, D.C., at the age of 14. She holds a bachelor's degree in international business from Strayer University, a project management executive certificate from Virginia Tech, and a master's degree in technology management from Georgetown University.

While at Georgetown, she was nominated to the Hoya Professional 30 class of 2018. Fernanda is a bilingual leader with over 15 years of combined experience in energy and utilities, and federal and private consulting.

She had the opportunity to become a member of Prospanica and later served on the chapter boards supporting and promoting higher education among Hispanics. She enjoys traveling around the world and pairing food with a nice glass of wine.

PROVE EVERYONE WRONG

TANIA TORRES-DELGADO

"Nothing inspired me more than doubters."

Ever since I can remember, I have always been underestimated. When you grow up in a predominantly Latino neighborhood with little resources, people assume you won't succeed. Nothing inspired me more than doubters.

When I was in second grade, my teacher asked the class to bring money from our native countries for show and tell. Being Puerto Rican, I naturally brought in a U.S. dollar. One of the American moms said to my mom, "I feel bad. Tania doesn't understand English. She brought in money from the U.S. instead of her native country." At the time, I didn't understand the gravity of her statement. It was later in life when I realized that I would encounter microaggressions and be underestimated for years to come.

When I was 14, I came home to find a note from my dad on the kitchen table saying he was leaving us. My mom became depressed, so I quickly became an adult and a caregiver. I juggled school, extracurricular activities, and the reality of what was going on at home.

One day, my mom's friend told her that I wasn't going to amount to anything because I was from a single-parent home and that I was going to be stuck in my mom's apartment for the rest of my life. That's all I needed to hear. I used that comment as fuel for the rest of my high school career and graduated with the fourth highest GPA in my class with acceptances to 11 colleges.

I chose to go to Columbia University. I had earned a scholarship from the American Chemical Society but could only access the funds if I studied chemistry. Even though deep down I knew I didn't want to study chemistry, I did because financial aid wasn't enough. Little did I know what that would really entail. To graduate with a chemistry degree, I had to dedicate over 70 credits to the sciences alone. Most other majors only required 50 credits. It was rough. I stayed up many nights until four o'clock in the morning, only to go to my campus security job at 7:30 and then class at nine.

During my sophomore year, my chemistry tutor told me that I had no hope of graduating with a chemistry concentration and that I should focus on something else. I thought, here we go again. I was tired of having to listen to others' opinions and was determined to prove everyone wrong. Instead of putting myself down, I put my blinders on and graduated in four years with my chemistry concentration.

It's no surprise to me that I'm not a chemist. I never wanted to be. What I learned was much more important, though. I learned that I am strong, resilient, and can do whatever I set my mind to do, regardless of my circumstances. I have countless other stories from adulthood where I was doubted because I was the youngest leader in the room, or the only Latina, but I now enjoy the challenge of proving people wrong.

BIOGRAPHY

Tania Torres-Delgado is a New Jersey native of Puerto Rican descent. She holds a bachelor's degree from Columbia University and currently works at Prudential, where she focuses on strategy and employee engagement.

She lives with her husband, who she has known since the age of 12, and her three-year-old daughter.

CLAUDIA TORRES-YÁÑEZ

"Experience is something you don't get until just after you need it."

It was 2007 and I was returning to work from maternity leave after having my third child. I had been in the workforce for nine years at a tech company, moving around in various accounting, audit, and finance roles. Until then, I was confident in the career decisions I had made and the skills and experience I had gained.

Sure, I hit a few bumps, but I felt like I was on track with my career. It had not been easy balancing the demands of work and home when my older two were toddlers and my career was just starting to progress. It was different returning to work after my youngest child was born. The decision I faced this time was how far outside my comfort zone to go. Could I let go of the known and the "safe," for the rewards and opportunity of the unknown?

I learned that sometimes (actually rarely) will you have all of the information you wish you had to decide. Many times, you will have to make the best decision you can with the information you do have. Unsure of what role I would return to, or what appealed to me, I received a call out of the blue from a former colleague about an opportunity. We had previously worked together in an accounting department, and she had made the move to an HR role a year or two before.

When she told me about the role, she told me she thought I would be good at it. I wondered. I didn't have any idea what the job was or the day-to-day responsibilities. I remember googling the job for a basic definition, that is how clueless I was about it! Since she was someone I deeply respected, I decided I should consider the job and interview for it.

I learned that the role required many of the same skills and knowledge I already had or could quickly gain. I also figured it was low risk, because the accounting function is always in need of support, closing of the books every month, every quarter...it literally never ends. If the HR role didn't work out, the accounting department would likely take me back. I could return, with my tail between my legs, for having failed in my little HR experiment.

2020 will mark thirteen years since I made that career decision. Little did I know all the growth and opportunity that would result from one decision, or how my skills would stand out and be much more valuable in HR.

I genuinely believe that playing it "safe" professionally, can be quite the opposite. I had to let go of my fears and insecurities, trust those who believed in me, and believe in myself. I used to be afraid of not having all the answers, not knowing what to do.

This quote by Steven Wright changed everything for me:

"Experience is something you don't get until just after you need it." Don't let fear hold you back!

BIOGRAPHY

Claudia Torres-Yáñez is currently the Senior Director of Total Rewards at SunPower Corporation. She was born and raised in Del Rio, Texas, and earned a master's in accounting degree from the University of Texas, Austin.

Claudia began her career at Motorola, where she found her calling in the HR Compensation and Benefits field after several years in the finance and accounting function.

She has earned professional licenses as a certified internal auditor and a CPA. She loves to travel, especially with her husband and three kids, and exercises regularly to take care of her physical and mental well-being.

THE CROSS-COUNTRY GAMBLE

LUIS A. VALDEZ-JIMENEZ

"Instead of being reactive and waiting for leadership opportunities to come to you, be proactive and seize leadership opportunities."

I was graduating with my Juris Doctor and MBA programs from the University of Wisconsin-Madison in my mid-twenties when I got an amazing job offer which required a move to Connecticut. I quickly realized that I knew nothing about Connecticut, had never been there, and I knew literally no one who lived there except for those I interviewed with.

I wondered how I would be noticed and advance in my career without the help of an established network? I was intimidated and I wondered whether or not to take the job. I decided to take the gamble and move to this completely unknown place, and it was one of the best decisions of my life.

I began researching young professional and industry organizations. I joined their mailing lists and social media pages ahead of time in order to see what kind of activities they are engaged in and the kinds of people who are involved. When I arrived, I began attending networking events regularly.

I eventually joined the Emerging Leaders Society, an official young professional's affinity group of the United Way of Central and Northeastern Connecticut, and the Connecticut chapter of Prospanica. These were exactly the kinds of organizations I wanted to join and volunteer in because they provided me with the opportunity to give back, network with other ambitious professionals, and get to know the area.

Often, when you are young and right out of school, your employer may be reluctant to give you leadership opportunities. Instead of being reactive and waiting for leadership opportunities to come to you, be proactive and seize leadership opportunities many local nonprofits may have available.

I eventually became the chair of the Emerging Leaders Society, the president of the Connecticut Chapter of Prospanica, and a board member of 360 Federal Credit Union which benefited me in numerous ways. I gained leadership experience in these organizations and I began getting noticed by local awards programs, media outlets, and other important people.

I won both the *Hartford Business Journal (HBJ) and Connecticut Magazine* "40 Under 40 Awards", and the Harvard Business Journal's Corporate Volunteer of the Year Award. After being recognized, a senior executive at my company reached out to me, and eventually I got a major promotion to work in his organization!

I learned that if you are going to a new place, do your research into local organizations you may be interested in. When you arrive, join them, and take on a leadership role. You will see that soon you will develop an impressive network of powerful and ambitious people, you will know the area, and your leadership skills will be developed in a way that will help you get noticed and advance in your career faster than you imagined.

I have been in Connecticut several years now and I have succeeded in an unexpected way. I plan to move back to Miami in late 2020 to be closer to family, and I will use the same strategy that worked so well in Connecticut to give back and thrive there.

BIOGRAPHY

Luis A. Valdez-Jimenez, J.D., MBA, is of Venezuelan/Salvadoran heritage and has lived throughout the U.S. He embraces ambition, adventure, and wants to make a meaningful impact in the community. He plans to launch new projects to promote language resources for professionals and organizations.

FROM DIFFICULT BATTLES, TRIUMPH ARISES

PATRICIA VARELA-GUEVARA & MAURICIO GUEVARA

"Aprende a nacer desde el dolor y a ser más grande que el más grande de los obstáculos."

In 2006, when a business deal turned sour with the wrong person, our family lost everything. This drove us (Patricia and Mauricio) to immigrate to Bedford Hills, New York, with our three daughters. Now imagine what it is to be pushed out of your comfort zone to a new place with an unknown language, culture, and rules?

That was completely bizarre and that's how we saw it at the time, especially without money in our pockets, since we had spent everything we had on our airfare tickets and rent for our first apartment in New York. We didn't know the language, or what kind of job we could get.

Since the day we moved here, we have knocked on every single door to find a job. Luckily, through the Katonah Community Center, we landed a part-time, overnight job cleaning the Katonah

Art Center while also working as house cleaners. Mauricio landed a job in construction, which is where he learned about woodworking.

Striving to provide a better future for our daughters, we saved money for their education while also trying to meet economic commitments in our country and support our future goals. I remember it clearly, when in 2015, after taking a trip upstate to buy wood for a side job that Mauricio took, we contemplated our dreams together.

We wanted to open our own business, and during that trip, we knew that we had to put all our faith into our dream and open up New England Antique Lumber. We had always been entrepreneurial, so instead of letting our failures discourage us, we let them be our biggest motivation to strive for success.

Being familiar with the area of Westchester County, we decided to invest everything we had and open up our shop in Mount Kisco, New York. Working from dawn to dusk for the past few years is what has made New England Antique Lumber succeed.

We have been extremely lucky to have landed in such a supportive community and have so many people open their doors to employ us in the past, whether it was as house cleaners or construction workers. We have worked extremely hard and put our heart in everything we did then and do today.

These past four years since opening our business we have learned one of the biggest lessons, which is that strength does not come from bodily capacity, but from the will of the soul. Pablo Neruda said to learn to be born from pain and to be greater than the greatest of obstacles. Arriving in the U.S. and facing the unknown was extremely challenging, but this country is full of opportunities for everyone.

If we did it, anyone else can do it. You are the only owner of your dreams, and you have to work immensely hard for it, but every tear, every sleepless night, every effort will be extremely rewarding once you achieve your American Dream, whether it is big or small. Work for it, feed your soul with hunger to succeed, and you will see how bright your future will shine.

BIOGRAPHY

Patricia and Mauricio, born and raised in Ecuador, immigrated to New York in 2006 with their three daughters. Ever since, they have worked hard in pursuit of their American Dream.

In 2015 they opened up New England Antique Lumber, Inc., a family-owned and operated business specializing in salvaging reclaimed timbers and creating custom wood pieces.

With just four years in the market, it has been recognized as the Best Reclaimed Wood Pieces Shop in Westchester, New York.

ENJOY LIFE-LONG LEARNING, TO DO WHAT YOU LOVE TO DO!

ED VARGAS

"Latinx people are Hispanic Stars and can work through challenges to be anything they want to be with the right motivation, planning, familia priorities, and a commitment to life-long learning."

I played football at Bellarmine College Preparatory and was offered a full scholarship for college but required knee surgery senior year. After two weeks recuperating, I was rushed to the hospital when I could not breath. I spent 36 hours on oxygen support and was treated for pneumonia.

The diagnosis confirmed blood clots passed through my heart and attached to my lungs. This moment instilled an awareness to be compassionate for people that are challenged, struggling with obstacles in life, or for their lives, such as COVID-19 patients on a respirator.

As I thought about my future, I set career goals for myself after getting my business and marketing degrees at Santa Clara

University. I wanted to be a management leader by the age of 30, to do business internationally, and to have an impact giving back and paying it forward.

I worked for a year before starting law school. Unfortunately, my mother was diagnosed with cancer and my father had a heart attack after my first year. I decided to work full-time and complete my JD degree at Santa Clara University in night classes. I was the first in my family to get an advanced degree.

I achieved my first career goal when I became a business executive at the age of 30. Starting in packaging sales, I became a product marketing manager, VP of sales, and marketing and corporate planner for Fortune 500 firms within six years.

I achieved my second career goal when I was recruited to become publisher, editor, and conference director for a start-up international B2B firm about nonwovens technology. I set up advertising sales agents in England and Belgium for European clients. We published a magazine, technical books, newsletters, and expanded a North America conference business to Tokyo, Japan, partnering with C-suite leaders.

International travel changed when my son was growing up. I developed my own strategic planning, marketing, and communications consulting firm. As a featured speaker at national conferences, I was invited to Harvard to participate in a roundtable on diversity. That became an article in the Harvard Business Review entitled, *A Question of Color: A Debate on Race in the U.S. Workplace.*

I am fulfilled paying it forward. I helped start High Tech Day (HTD) with AT&T's HACEMOS ERG members, i.e., STEM workshops for local high school students at AT&T facilities. HTD became the flagship national annual event for the last 21 years, with more than 2,500 students from 30+ cities in the U.S., Puerto Rico, and Mexico.

As AT&T HACEMOS ERG National EVP-Community Outreach, I launched HACEMOS Latino Diversity Stories on YouTube to generate awareness of members' success stories focusing on what we have in common.

Don't expect a lifetime career because you have a degree. Latinx people are Hispanic Stars and can work through challenges to be anything they want to be with the right motivation, planning, *familia* priorities, and a commitment to life-long learning.

Throughout my career, I learned to live that way every day. I encourage you to seek life balance, prioritizing time with family, and overcoming obstacles to find happiness.

BIOGRAPHY

Ed Vargas is head of D&I ERGs/Latinx practice leads at ctrfactor.com, and reignited his own consulting group, Vargas and Associates.

He is a mentor at the Miller Center for Social Entrepreneurship at Santa Clara University, the SF Silicon Valley Hispanic Star Hub Lead, and is passionate about paying it forward.

Ed held C-suite roles in packaging and international publishing corporations and has taken on other roles to remain in the San Francisco Bay Area.

His nonprofit experience includes Director of Communications, Media Relations, World Affairs Council of Northern California, Chairperson of the Community Advisory Panel for the board of KQED, and President of the Hispanic Community Foundation.

FROM I AM NOT ENOUGH TO I AM TOTALLY WORTH IT!

CLAUDIA VAZQUEZ

"Surround yourself with those who believe in the beauty of your dreams."

My beginning may be different from other Latinas living in the U.S. today. My parents met and got married in California, where I was born. However, when I was one year old, we moved to Guadalajara Jalisco, Mexico.

Between the age of nine and now, I have lived in seven cities within Mexico, the U.S., and Canada. At the age of 24, my husband and I decided to permanently move to California for several reasons. First, I could finish my bachelor's degree, which I had always dreamed of doing, but hadn't due to finances and the relocations, and second, to live in the land of opportunities.

Upon arriving in Pasadena, I visited the closest community college campus and took several placement tests. My English score was very low, so the counselor recommended multiple English classes. To make a long story short, I ultimately realized that unless I had a clear goal and a plan to achieve it, I would not succeed.

Therefore, I created a master plan and began to diligently work towards it. It took me six years to finish my bachelor's degree while working full time, being pregnant with our first child, and managing the purchase of our first home.

I also followed my calling to help others succeed, by volunteering as an ESL teacher and a citizenship instructor. More than 80 Hispanic students achieved their U.S. citizenship by attending my classes at a local community center.

The feelings of not being "enough" and not even "college material" came to mind several times throughout those six years, whenever I couldn't understand certain economic concepts, such as statistical regression analysis, or computer coding.

Or when I applied to an amazing Fortune 500 company and was hired at a 20 percent lower salary because I had not finished my degree. I did not quit or blame anyone, though. I did not stop pursuing my ultimate dream. On the contrary, I persevered, pushed through, got up every morning, remained positive, and was determined and diligent. It is all about grit and attitude!

At the age of 30, we had our first son. Forty days later, I graduated with a degree in psychology. The transgenerational cycle was broken; I became the first one in my family to graduate from college! Since then, I have received multiple promotions and growth opportunities, as well as national and international recognitions for the impact I have had in the community and for being a diversity and inclusion leader wherever I go.

I found my passion and have achieved many of my dreams!

But I could not have done it without the support of my husband, my family, friends, encouraging managers, and co-workers. It takes a village. Surround yourself with those who believe in the beauty of your dreams! I am Claudia, I am a Hispanic Star, and my true journey is just getting started.

BIOGRAPHY

Claudia Vazquez, MAOM, LSSBB, has 20 years of insurance experience. Currently, she is a Director, Product Management, of Prudential's Group Insurance. For several years, Claudia supervised Prudential's Africa, Europe, and Latin American region compliance teams.

Prior to joining Prudential, she had leadership positions at State Farm, Unum, and Cigna. Claudia earned a B.A. in Psychology and an M.A. in Organizational Management. She holds certifications in project management, Six Sigma, and as an Agile professional.

Most recently, Claudia founded Elevink, a consulting practice that focuses on elevating inclusion of underrepresented talented individuals, diversity and inclusion strategy, education, recruitment, and leadership development.

THE POWER OF BRAGGING FOR THE RIGHT CAUSE

CAROLINA M. VEIRA

"There is no limit to what we can accomplish together."

I was born and raised in the vibrant country of Ecuador, famous for the Galapagos Islands, Panama hats, flowers, Guayaquil, bananas, and the equator. Being Ecuadorian, my family shaped my personality. I was, from a young age, an overly optimistic, expressive, and passionate dreamer who wanted to do it all by becoming a singer, actress, writer, tour guide, missionary, teacher, activist, and CEO.

It's a world where you are told to dream less, be more realistic, be one thing only, while talking less, and focusing on the bottom line. Disregarding basic human needs are oftentimes an afterthought. So, I decided not to pay attention to these standards and trust my instinct. I decided to believe in myself and that I could do and be anything, if I work hard, trust God, and my intrinsic belief that to be happy, I had to be kind to myself and serve others.

I could hear those voices telling me why I was not good

enough, that I needed to look different, sound different, think differently. And in those moments of self-doubt, I wrote letters to myself reminding me of why I was worthy of success and happiness. Over the years my "why" went from who I wanted to be to whom I wanted to help, to the impact I wanted to generate in the world. I slowly realized that to see the change, I needed to be the change. I decided I was going to become that voice to speak for those who have none, who need to be represented; those who need to be seen, heard, and valued.

It is my belief that our voices and our personal stories have unlimited power and need to be shared with the world. Our words are meant to empower those around us, to lift each other up, to nurture our differences, our uniqueness, and our diversity. As a community, we all need to talk more about what we bring to the table, about our accomplishments and our success stories, because not only do we deserve to talk about these stories, but many out there need to hear them, to believe they also have a shot at fulfilling their dreams.

We can be and do a million things, not only one. This is what I call bragging for the right cause. Our combined efforts make us all a stronger force to be reckoned with and help open doors that would otherwise not open.

My superpower is my identity. I am the daughter of Johnny Veira and Aida Corrales and sister to Johnny and Osman. I am a mom, a communicator, a leader, a volunteer. I am a proud Hispanic American who is passionate about kindness, empathy, and the power of community. I believe we can be one thing and all things. ***We can change the world one story at a time.***

BIOGRAPHY

Carolina M. Veira is an authentic leader, financial strategist, and diversity and inclusion advocate, with a passion for the advancement and empowerment of Hispanics, women, and other minority groups across various stages in their lives.

With nearly 15 years of demonstrated success in creating community initiatives and strategic partnerships, Carolina now works to strengthen and expand the mission and impact across South Florida of IMC Health Medical Centers and The Hispanic Star Miami.

Carolina earned a double bachelor of science degree from D'Youville College in business and accounting and an MBA. She is Ecuadorian-American currently residing in Miami.

CULTURE & LANGUAGE ARE GIFTS TO BE CHERISHED

MARIA BARTOLOME WINANS

"Language is the roadmap of a culture. It tells you where its people come from, and where they are going."

I was born in Santiago Chile and immigrated to North Carolina when I was only ten years old. My father was a research scientist, and his latest opportunity was to conduct biochemistry research at Duke University. This was a thrilling new chapter in my family's life, and although the United States was a strange new world, I knew that great things awaited us.

My mother taught me that culture and language were a gift, and that I must cherish both. Few can understand how it felt to be a young Latina growing up in the southern part of the United States. I came here not knowing any English at all but learned by watching endless hours of Sesame Street until I was fluent.

At home, my parents maintained conversation with one another in Español to further establish the importance of culture at home, where it mattered most. Afterall, as Rita Mae Brown says, "Language is the roadmap of a culture. It tells you where its people come from, and where they are going."

My family remained united by our strong sense of heritage. As a young girl, this often confused me because at school and amongst my peers, I was always considered different; I looked different, I spoke different, and I thought different. Because of this, it was not always easy for me to see that my differences were what kept me so close to the culture that molded me into who I am today. Over time, I learned that my differences gave me perspective, and perspective is one of the most powerful assets that you can bring to any table.

When I started with IBM straight out of school, I was embraced and empowered by my peers to weave my love for my heritage into my actual career by getting involved with matters of diversity and inclusion at work. IBM has a strong history with D&I and has committed itself since the time of its founding to creating an equal opportunity workplace for people with all kinds of diverse backgrounds.

IBM has taken me on many different adventures in a variety of different roles, countries, and experiences. But the platform that IBM has given me to empower the future of Hispanics in technology has perhaps been the greatest adventure of them all. I learned how to differentiate myself from others by bringing my best self to work every single day and letting my unique perspective shine.

As my career progressed, I made it my top priority to share

that focus with other young women and people of color through mentorship, panel discussions dedicated to D&I, and my work as co-chair of IBM's Hispanic Council.

My mother was absolutely right--culture and language are a gift, gifts that are meant to be taken care of and displayed with pride. I have dedicated myself to the progression and empowerment of diverse people and hope to encourage them to continue to embrace their differences as pillars of strength and perspective for the future of our world.

BIOGRAPHY

Maria Bartolome Winans is the Chief Marketing Officer for IBM Americas, leading all aspects of marketing with responsibility for marketing-sourced revenue and demand generation. Some of Maria's key roles have included strategic initiatives and leading teams across business analytics, collaboration solutions, industry solutions, data management, PC company and digital channel.

Maria serves as co-chair of IBM's Hispanic Executive Council and is an outspoken and proud advocate for the Hispanic community. Maria holds several accolades from being named one of the Top 10 Corporate Latina Executives of the Year by *LATINA Style*, to also being awarded the ASPIRA Association's Corporate Leadership Award.

ON RESILIENCE AND ADAPTATION

MARGARITA WOMACK

"I am a citizen of the world, melding the various facets of my identity to build an empanada empire."

It was the year 2000 and I was 20 years old. Ready for the new millennium, my life in my hometown of Bogotá, Colombia, was just perfect. I was halfway through my sophomore year of college, though as often is the case in Bogotá, I was still living at home with my family. I was lost in love in my first serious relationship and, naïvely, I believed eternal happiness was a given.

But Colombia has been the scenario for rippling violence for more than 50 years. One of the main players in this conflict, FARC *(Fuerzas Armadas Revolucionarias de Colombia)* attempted to extort my family. The threats quickly started escalating. I will never forget the roaring voice on the answering machine. "Mrs., if at 18 hours you have not followed our instructions, we will declare you and your family a military objective."

I was forced out of my home country and my life changed forever when I moved to the U.S. I was resolved to create a chance to grow and grab the opportunity to reinvent myself. I focused on my education, finished my undergraduate degree, and continued with a PhD, following my passion for science and the inner workings of the natural world. During my time in graduate school, I met my husband and we had our first son, soon followed by two more.

After spending a few years teaching in the metro DC area, I had the opportunity to once more reinvent myself. I went back to school, this time for an MBA, and started my own company, Latin Goodness Foods. It's first brand was Maspanadas. Now three years old, Latin Goodness Foods makes modern empanadas for the hospitality and retail industry along the east coast and is expanding.

It has been a challenge to balance so many roles: wife, mother, and female entrepreneur, but it is all somehow coming along. A bit of luck and good energy have been essential, but I owe my success to an incredibly supportive husband who takes more than his share of house chores and childcare. I also rely on many others who have believed in and fueled my dreams.

I now have spent over half my life in the United States. I am part Colombian, part American. Part of me belongs in Bogotá, where I was raised. Part of me belongs in Bethesda, Maryland, where I carved a niche for family and my business that now I call home.

However, people hear my accent in the U.S. and often ask where I come from. I get the same question while on vacation in Colombia. Apparently, I also have some sort of accent when I speak Spanish. In a way I belong here, I belong there, but I don't fully belong anywhere. I am a citizen of the world, melding the various facets of my identity to build an empanada empire.

BIOGRAPHY

Margarita Womack is a business executive and entrepreneur. She holds a B.S. from Tulane University, a PhD from Princeton University, and an MBA from Georgetown University.

She is the founder of Latin Goodness Foods, a company bringing fusion South American street foods to fuel life in the fast lane.

Previously, Dr. Womack was involved in science education and research through teaching K-12, leading the development of a nonprofit to foster science in her home country, Colombia, and carrying out primary research at Princeton University.

THE PAST HAS A SHADOW

NUVIA YESENIA

"Rather than allowing your past to be your crutch, influence it so it can be your engine."

I used to think that only those who are in jail and behind metal bars are imprisoned. But I was wrong, because I was imprisoned while being free. I let my past take over my present, which jeopardized my future. I was a slave to my negative thoughts and therefore, I developed a pessimistic attitude. I kept torturing myself with the voices of shame and guilt.

The voice of shame was here to remind me that I was useless for always giving up. The voice of guilt was here to engrave in my mind that my past actions were horrible and deceiving. These voices left me feeling helpless in a path that I thought had no way out for me. There were many painful experiences that I encountered as a child that led me into a chaotic and traumatic adulthood.

As a child, I saw myself singing and playing the guitar at big concerts. I saw myself being a New York Times best-selling author. I saw myself triumph and help others along the way. Then, I was told many times by loved ones that I was weak, and that I lacked potential. I was hurt by the ones I trusted. Their words became my truth and I began to walk on a path of excuses and self-criticism. I began to commit mistake after mistake until I no longer recognized myself. I allowed the voices of the past to shatter those dreams into pieces.

With time, my dreams stayed only dreams. I was abandoned by my parents, family, and friends. I felt alone, scared, and unworthy. I became an alcoholic, and when alcohol could not hush the voices, I began to consume drugs. I had no clue of the drastic pain I was causing myself. I had transformed myself into the shadow of my past.

One day I decided that it was time for me to stop being a victim. The moment I made up my mind, a miracle happened. I changed my perspective on my past and found a way out. Rather than seeing it as a horrible thing, I began to embrace it.

I then noticed that inspiration began to whisper in my ear. I began to play music and write stories. All the dreams I had of becoming a great writer and musician were now in my hands. I began to cherish my body; therefore, I no longer intoxicate her with abusive substances. I have been able to liberate myself from the chains that kept me in a miserable state.

Rather than allowing your past to be your crutch, influence it so it can be your engine. My painful past is now my engine because it pushes me to work for what I had always dreamed of. I had allowed my past to define me, but now I have learned to use it to create a better version of myself. It is never too late to live the life of your dreams.

I no longer look back with regret or pity. Now I only look back to grasp ideas so I can write my own masterpiece.

BIOGRAPHY

Nuvia Yesenia is a writer and musician. She is the author of *"My New Veganning,"* a memoir written to inspire others. She is a singer, drummer, guitar, and bass player. She is a songwriter and shares her music with others. She lives with purpose and her goal is to leave a footprint on this Earth.

¡DALE, QUE TÚ PUEDES!"

CHANEL ZAPATA

"Never doubt yourself and make it happen."

Growing up in San Juan, Puerto Rico, there are not a lot of things you can complain about. You have a beautiful island, culture, and history, but most importantly, you have the best people. Like many Hispanic, Latino, or Latinx families, main activities happen at the grandmother's house, and mine was no exception.

Every gathering, Thanksgiving, Christmas, New Year's, birthday, and *Noches de San Juan* occurred under one roof, and being the only granddaughter had a lot of advantages like asking for specific food, listening to your favorite song on repeat, and getting pretty much whatever you wanted.

I was raised by an exceptional single mother, the most intelligent little brother, aunts and uncles that were always there, and the most amazing grandparents you could ever ask for, and even though I was privileged with all those blessings, I decided to take a leap of faith to follow my dreams and go to college in the United States.

My family always reminded me to not take no for an answer and to always believe there was a way to achieve things, just like my mother did when she completed her bachelor's degree with not one, but two children.

As I moved away from home and settled into Athens, Ohio, that lesson never escaped me and thank God it didn't. Here is where I got sick for the first time and I did not have my mom to snuggle me, or when I simply too homesick to attend classes. This is also when I encountered episodes of racism and xenophobia for the first time.

What I remember is the pain, the humiliation, and the frustration of feeling that there was nothing you could do about it. However, there was. Like they always told me, I could achieve anything that I wanted, and, in this case, it was to continue school and finish my courses until we could find another solution.

Three years later, I graduated from my undergraduate program and was ready to take on a new chapter--graduate school. Nobody knew that this was preparing me for an even bigger challenge, which was being forced to move out of Puerto Rico due to Hurricane Maria.

As I sit here writing this, I can tell you that the biggest lesson was the one imparted on me since my childhood. Now, I can weave a piece of it into the story and continue to share it with a new generation. Never forget where you came from, always be grateful, never doubt yourself, and make it happen.

BIOGRAPHY

Chanel Zapata was born and raised in San Juan, Puerto Rico. She holds a Bachelor of Science in Sports Management from The University of Tampa and a master of science in sport law and business from Arizona State University.

Currently, she is planning on visiting different countries, spending lots of time with her dog, Vida, and increasing representations of marginalized communities within the sport of baseball.

ABOUT THE AUTHOR

Claudia Romo Edelman is a social entrepreneur, an inspiring data-driven speaker, and a determined catalyst for positive change. As a recognized speaker, media contributor and advocate, Claudia is a leader for diversity, inclusion and equity, focused on unifying the U.S. Hispanic community, and promoting sustainability and purpose-driven activities, particularly within brands, tech, and the creative industries.

With an extraordinary background with global organizations, including the United Nations, UNICEF, and the World Economic Forum, she has collaborated and worked on humanitarian causes for 25 years with organizations such as (RED), the United Nations High Commissioner for Refugees (UNHCR), and the Global Fund to fight AIDS, tuberculosis, and malaria.

Claudia is Founder of the We Are All Human Foundation, a New York-based nonprofit foundation, dedicated to advancing the agenda of diversity, inclusion and equity through developing and hosting regional and local events, conducting research and developing research pieces/publications, creating content, and corporate activation.

She enjoys sports, traveling with her husband and two children, and speaks six languages.

ABOUT THE PUBLISHER

Jacqueline Camacho is a visionary social entrepreneur who has created an enterprise of inspiration. Her keen sense of service coupled with the vision to bring good to the world have led her to create two successful, award-winning companies, establish two nonprofit organizations, publish over 20 books of her own, create many products, and hold dozens of events around the world in just the past decade.

She is often referred to as a "dream catcher," as her strategies have supported thousands of women, authors and young ladies to live a life of significance. Jacqueline's quest to be a servant leader extends to every area of her life. She has shared her inspiration in four continents and aligned with some of the most powerful brands to elevate others. At only 37 years of age, she has achieved what most would not do in an entire lifetime. Being a cancer survivor sparked a sense of urgency to serve and transcend.

Jacqueline believes that magix (yes, a made-up word that means magic x 10) is the intersection of profit and impact.

She is one of the few Latina sports airplane pilots in the United States.

Jacqueline believes that "taking off is optional, landing on your dreams is mandatory."